WAKE UP CALL

WAKE UP CALL

LESSONS FROM THE ALS ICE BUCKET CHALLENGE FOR NONPROFIT SOCIAL MEDIA

DEB FINCH

NEW DEGREE PRESS

COPYRIGHT © 2020 DEB FINCH

All rights reserved.

WAKE UP CALL

Lessons from the ALS Ice Bucket Challenge for Nonprofit Social Media

ISBN 978-1-63676-539-6 *Paperback*

978-1-63676-091-9 *Kindle Ebook*

978-1-63676-092-6 *Ebook*

Dedication

To my dad, Joseph P. Davock, who always inspired me by reading and surrounding us with books to read. To Jim Cline, who believed from the beginning that I could write this book. To my children, Joe, Carter, Sam, and Harry, who probably can't wait for me to be done talking about writing this book!

I also dedicate this book to my friend, Melanie St. Croix, and her willingness to share her story of life with ALS. You inspire and remind me every day of what it means to live a life filled with love.

And to my friend, Terry O'Connor, who has shown unbelievable strength and knows what it means to have the love and encouragement of family and friends. You have been there for me in good times and bad, and your unwavering friendship means so much to me.

TABLE OF CONTENTS

ACKNOWLEDGEMENTS

While writing this book, I had the support of so many colleagues, friends, and family. I couldn't have done it without you! I will be forever grateful as I tackled a topic that has been in my mind for the last six years. Your feedback and your contributions helped me achieve my goal. Thank you for inspiring my drive, which gave me the confidence that helped make this book a reality.

Special thanks to my beta readers, Allison Cline, Jim Cline, Joan Crooker, Louise Durand, Karen Hvizda, and Belinda Juran. Your thoughtful suggestions and editing were so helpful, and you kept me going through the journey.

I am so appreciative of the opportunity to interview people, who willingly gave their time and shared their knowledge. This book couldn't have happened without you!

Richard Blain
Lorna Boucher
Angel Brunelle
Julia Campbell
Elizabeth Cannon
Brian Frederick
Colleen Gordon
David Hall

Ron Hoffman
Teresa Jardon
Eva Montibello
Carrie Munk
LZ Nunn
Spencer Ross
Mark Yim

Thank you to a wonderful group of supporters who helped me ensure this book would happen. Your belief that I would actually get this written drove me on some of the hardest days. I will always be grateful for your encouragement.

Lisa Armstrong
Eileen Augustus
Mary Barrett
Michael Beers
Chris Bendann
Rick Blain
Ruth Boehl
Holly Butler
James Canning
Erin Caples
Sandra Carriker
Laura Christianson
Annie Ciaraldi
Michael Ciuchta
Tina Clement
Allison Cline
Jim Cline
John Cline
Michelle Costello
Allison Cree
Joan Crooker
Joanne & Adam Dunbar
Marijane Davock
Jon deAlderete
Joanna DelMonico
Louise Durand
Jim Dyment
Amy Erickson
John Feudo
Joe Finch
Sam Finch
Harry Finch
Tawnya Finkel
Megan Foster
John Geraci
Gianna Geraci
Bob Gilman
Carolyn Gregoire
Lisa Gwaizda
Judy Haley
David Hall
Karen Hvizda
Collette Joliffe
Ralph Jordan

Belinda Juran
Karen Kane
Sal Kapadia
Erin Keaney
Jim Keenan
Eric Koester
Janet Lambert Moore
Matt Lawson
Diane Lefebvre
David Levine
Jennifer Linatsis
Bea Alice Loos
MaryRose Loring
Patrick Lotti
Ashwin Mehta
Tracy Moore
Joey Moore
Milissa Moynihan
Donna Mullin
Jenny Murphy
Margaret Murray
Rosemary Noon
Jean O'Brien
Sharon O'Donnell
Beth Patrick
Melissa & Stephen Pennell
Michael Penta
Joanne Pesnell
Ha Pho
Chris Porter
Sovanna Pouv
Karyn Puleo
Shaima Ragab
Andre Ragel
Mary Ellen Ramsey
Donna Richards
Diana Robarge
Jodi Robinson
Steven Rogers
Spencer Ross
Carter Sartell
Anne Sayers
Kelly Skelton
Allyssa St. Croix
Erica Steckler
Melinda Stewart
Li Sun
Sean Thibodeau
John Ting
Tatiana Tompkins
Robin Toof
Bethanne Welch
Amy Werner
Jim Wilde
Kevin Willett
Barbara Williams
Lance Williams
Martina Witts
Amy Woo
Christine Wyman
Yi Yang
Joanne Yestramski
Mark Yim
William Zousas

This book would not be possible without the creative development of the Creator Institute by Georgetown University professor Eric Koester, the help of New Degree Press, and the enthusiastic support of Head of Publishing Brian Bies. Allison Tovey and Sarah Lobrot, you offered guidance and patience in your role as editors, always knowing when to push just a little bit harder and offering plenty of praise along the way. I truly looked forward to our weekly meetings. Thank you all for this amazing experience.

INTRODUCTION

Do you remember the first time you saw someone dump a bucket of ice over their head on social media? They were probably taking part in the ALS Ice Bucket Challenge. Were you intrigued, shocked, or impressed? Think about how you felt when videos of people doing this began to appear. The idea of emptying a bucket of ice water over our heads was, no pun intended, shocking! Did you take the challenge?

In the summer of 2014, an organic movement began that would change the way nonprofits look at social media as a tool for marketing: The ALS Ice Bucket Challenge. This created a call to action to pour a bucket of ice-cold water over your head to raise awareness and funds for research and care of people with ALS. The ALS Ice Bucket Challenge went viral on social media, and millions of people took part in this experience! Each participant was asked to nominate three people to take the challenge.[1]

---

1 Amanda Trejos, "Ice Bucket Challenge: 5 things you should know," *USA Today*, July 3, 2017.

The Ice Bucket Challenge was the first time many people globally learned about ALS, also known as Lou Gehrig's disease, and the fight to find viable treatments and a cure. If you didn't accept the challenge, you were supposed to donate one hundred dollars to ALS research. It was an incredible success: "In the summer of 2014, the ALS Ice Bucket Challenge inspired 17 million people to upload videos and raised $115 million for the ALS Association."[2]

It was a wake-up call to the world and a transformative moment for nonprofits. No longer could social media be relegated to "we'll get to it when we can"; rather, it became a new way to tell the stories and missions of so many causes. In an interview with David Hall, currently associate vice president of external relations at Greater Lawrence Family Health Center located in Lawrence, Massachusetts, he said, "I don't think we did much on social media before the Ice Bucket Challenge. The Challenge really helped people to start thinking about how they could do social media fundraising, and how companies could utilize it for social good."[3] Hall, with a strong background in fundraising, noted that the executive team at Lowell General Hospital in Lowell, Massachusetts had taken the ALS Ice Bucket Challenge that summer and encouraged LGH employees, along with other health care businesses, to take up the challenge. Hall remembers the natural connection of ALS with the hospital and how excited people were to participate.

---

2 "ALS Ice Bucket Challenge Year-End Update: Over $94 Million in Commitments Since 2014," ALS Association, Accessed June 24, 2020.

3 David Hall (in his previous role as senior manager of philanthropy, volunteer & concierge Services at Lowell General Hospital in Lowell, Massachusetts) in discussion with the author.

When the ALS Ice Bucket Challenge began, I was a little skeptical. Would all these people donate money to ALS, or were they just using it as a way to be "cool," pun intended, on social media? No one ever asked me to do the challenge, and I confess I felt a little bit left out. "Why not me?" I wondered. At that time, I didn't know much about ALS or its devastating effects on people's lives.

Today, I do know about ALS. My friend, Melanie St. Croix, was diagnosed with ALS in 2018. Melanie is one of the friendliest, most helpful people I have ever met. We were first introduced on the board of the Lowell Association for the Blind, which provides services for the blind and visually impaired in the greater Merrimack Valley of Massachusetts. We both care deeply about raising awareness for and improving the lives of those who have lost their vision. When Melanie served as president of the board of directors, I was able to see the leadership she provided to the organization and her heartfelt concern for our blind and visually impaired clients. After a board meeting, she would often offer to drive home one of the board members, who was blind, so he would not have to worry about finding a ride. Her caring and kindness made everyone who knew her respect and admire her.

I'm including Melanie's story, using her own words, in this book because I think it is helpful to be able to see and feel why the ALS Ice Bucket Challenge is so important. I hope you will read her story and realize you or someone you loved could be diagnosed with ALS or another life-changing disease at any time. The challenge is a strong reminder of why it is so important nonprofits exist. If nonprofits want to educate, inform, and gain new volunteers and donors, using social media strategically is critical to getting the message out to the public.

WHY NOW?

I know everyone learns better when they can connect with a topic. I have been involved in nonprofits as both a volunteer and a director on several boards. In addition, I homeschooled my four children until they went to college. This path led me to a teaching career at the University of Massachusetts Lowell. For a long time, I've felt the need for a story that would engage students in my Marketing for Nonprofits class at the university, to help them better understand the role of marketing in nonprofits, and also let them know about career paths within nonprofit organizations. I try to make my classes interesting and interactive, with real hands-on learning opportunities and a chance to make a difference in the lives of others.

I use a common read in several of the classes I teach, for which all the students read the same book at the same time. The books always grab students' attention, even those who say they don't like to read! The two books I use routinely are Diana Kander's *All In Startup: Launching a New Idea When Everything Is on the Line* and Wendy Kopp's *One Day, All Children...: The Unlikely Triumph of Teach For America And What I Learned Along the Way.* I've searched for a book that tells a story about nonprofit marketing, but without success. I'd hoped someone else would write a book that would work, but then I met Eric Koester, Georgetown University professor and founder of the Creator Institute, at an entrepreneurship conference. He convinced me *I* should write the book. He developed a program that led students and others through the book-writing process over the course of a year. I was immediately intrigued, as I thought of the students I teach at UMass Lowell and how much they would enjoy a course like this one! However, I knew that in order to bring it to the university, I would need to complete the experience myself.

BOOKS INSPIRE ME

What I like about both books referenced above is how the authors engage the reader with strong story lines and cliff-hangers that make you want to keep reading. Often as you're reading, you start to care about the characters, which is enough for you to want to learn more.

It is interesting that Kander's book is fictional, but it is based on fact. The information is the equivalent of an entry-level Introduction to Entrepreneurship textbook without all the boring stuff! In fact, this is why Kander wrote it that way: She felt entrepreneurship textbooks were dull to read. Critical to her book was learning to identify the problem you are solving, along with who is your customer and what are their needs? You can't learn about starting a business without understanding your potential customer. You have to talk to them *before* you start your business.[4] I have great admiration for Kander and her work, and I use her podcasts and YouTube videos in my classes.

---

4 Diana Kander, *All In Startup: Launching a New Idea When Everything is on the Line*, (Hoboken: John Wiley & Sons, Inc., 2014.)

Kopp's book is nonfiction, but she writes in a way that makes you want to find out what happens next, perhaps because her book is such a compelling story of determination and perseverance. Kopp started Teach For America based on her senior thesis, a requirement of all graduates from Princeton University. When Kopp first arrived at college, she felt her high school had prepared her well. Her roommate, however, struggled. Kopp didn't think it was fair that while she had been fortunate enough to live in a town with a higher average income, students who did not have this advantage were unable to receive the same level of college preparation. This experience led her to think about how to improve education in under resourced school districts.[5] My students like this story because they are wise enough to recognize that this inequity happens across the country and because they can see themselves reflected in Kopp's uncertainty about what to do when she graduates. They also like Kopp's willingness to jump in and get the job done, no matter what it takes.

I want to write a book that is engaging for readers and tells a meaningful story. If students, nonprofit personnel, volunteers, and board members can identify with the book, want to keep reading, and apply the tips and suggestions, that will be enough for me. I believe we can learn so much from reading stories about topics that stir passion in ourselves and others. No matter what you do, if you love it, it will never feel like work. The nonprofit sector needs people who are eager and passionate about making change, and I want students to see

---

5 Wendy Kopp, *One Day, All Children...: The Unlikely Triumph Of Teach For America And What I Learned Along The Way*, (Cambridge: Perseus Books, 2013.)

they can use a skill like marketing to make a difference in the lives of others.

WHY NONPROFITS?

You might be asking why I'm limiting this book to nonprofits. Don't all businesses benefit from social media? The answer is yes, but I want to focus on nonprofits because

- The people in nonprofits are passionate about their mission.
- Nonprofits can make a difference in people's lives.
- I have always been interested in nonprofits and what they do.
- I believe students who learn about them find inspiration in their work and sometimes even discover career paths they had never considered.
  - Working in a nonprofit with clients, constituents, volunteers, and donors is different than working in a for-profit company that focuses only on customers.
- I want nonprofits to understand that **"'More Posts' Is Not a Strategy!" #MPINS**

I am fortunate to teach classes that introduce students to the business side of nonprofits. In the education world, we use the term "service-learning" for students who work with community and nonprofit organizations on projects that involve helping solve an organization's problems. Service-learning is real-life learning, and it's quite different than just learning material in a classroom with no connection to how it will help a business! Service-learning incorporates experiential and classroom learning and helps students see the impact they can make on an organization. I have found service-learning to be an incredibly valuable experience in students' lives. I have students who learn from taking a service-learning course that they want to pursue a career in nonprofits because they want to do work that brings meaning to their lives!

As professors, we often discuss how we can determine students' learning outcomes. Much of what we teach and experience is not easy to assess, though qualitative and quantitative methods are certainly available. Assessment is an integral part of nonprofit programs, too! But these assessments are usually done in a short time frame. Measuring long-term effects on a person's life is hard. The story of how I became interested in helping people with visual impairments (and how that interest led to my service-learning experiences for students) may explain both my passion for these topics and the challenge of predicting what might have a long-term effect on a person's life:

> When I was eleven years old, I read Nan Gilbert's book *A Dog for Joey*.[6] It tells the story of a boy raising a seeing-eye dog under the stern eye of his father, who had moved the family from their farm in Iowa to a town in Oregon. I was an avid reader as a child, and this was the first time I had read anything about seeing eye dogs. That story stayed with me throughout my teen years and sparked an interest in people with vision issues. When I had to decide what to do for college, I knew I couldn't face four more years of school. Through my cousin, I learned about

6 Nan Gilbert, *A Dog for Joey*, (New York: Harper & Row, 1967.)

Fisher Junior College and a program at the New England College of Optometry, where I could study to become an optometric technician. Upon graduation, I went to work for Doctors Bournakel and Beale in Lewiston, Maine, a practice that had a specialty in low vision. While I was there, I worked with several low vision patients and grew to love working with them and seeing how different equipment and treatment could make such a difference in their lives.

After a year, I moved to Massachusetts to attend the University of Lowell and study physics, with the hope of attending optometry school and becoming an optometrist. In the end, I didn't end up going, but I had added to my skill set and had become an ophthalmic technician, working with ophthalmologists in their medical practice. The wife of one of the doctors was on the board of directors of the Lowell Association for the Blind, and she asked me if I would be interested in serving on the board. It was a turning point for me. Forty years later, I am still there as director emerita.

That was my first experience with nonprofits, but I went on to volunteer and serve on the boards of several nonprofit organizations and foundations. I could see the people involved were passionate about their mission and wanted to help others, and I knew I wanted that in my life, too.

And all because I read a book when I was eleven years old!

You never know what will trigger something in someone that may have a lifelong positive influence on their life and the lives of others.

WHY KEEP READING?

You might be wondering, "What's in this book for me?" If you are involved in nonprofit organizations in any way, this book will show you why you need to link your social media to your overall marketing strategy, and I'll give you some tools and tips to help make that happen. This book is intended to help nonprofit administrators, staff, boards of directors, volunteers, and students learn how to use social media to best further the mission of the organization. Even if you already use social media marketing, I offer specific ways you can use the culture of your organization to help everyone associated with it understand that they are marketers, too.

Come along with me on this journey to see *how nonprofits can change their thinking about social media and how they can maximize its potential.* What I have found has changed the way I see the future of nonprofit organizations.

PART 1

LAYING THE GROUNDWORK

CHAPTER 1

MELANIE'S STORY

You never think it can happen to you! I doubt a single person reading this has not been touched or have a love one who has been touched by illness or disability. Whether it's ALS, cancer, blindness, stroke, or heart attack, all of these and more serve as a reminder that life brings unexpected and often unwanted events. As the old saying goes, "Life throws you curveballs when you least expect them." How you deal with those curveballs is what makes a difference.

ALS "is a progressive neurodegenerative disease that affects nerve cells in the brain and the spinal cord."[7] ALS affects motor neurons, resulting in loss of the ability to talk, walk, eat, and breathe. ALS has no cure and limited treatment at this time.[8] A diagnosis of ALS is progressive and terminal.

Before I started writing this book, I knew I wanted to include the story of how ALS can affect a person's life. One reason is to help you, the reader, gain insight into how the ALS Ice

---

7 "What is ALS?" alsa.org, Accessed April 6, 2020.

8 "What is ALS?"

Bucket Challenge changed the public knowledge and awareness of the disease through social media. The second reason is because I knew reading my friend Melanie's experience with ALS would help you better understand the need for nonprofits in society to provide services, education, and programs to those affected.

Melanie's story starts the journey from her early impressions of the ALS Ice Bucket Challenge before she was diagnosed and continues through to her life now. Throughout the book, I'll provide more of Melanie's experience and her fight for independence and quality of life. In telling this, I hope you will realize that stories can tell powerful messages of hope and resilience. Stories help us make the connection between learning and experience, which is just what social media should be doing for your nonprofit!

MELANIE'S LIFE AT THE TIME OF THE ALS ICE BUCKET CHALLENGE, PRE-DIAGNOSIS

When the ALS Ice Bucket Challenge appeared on social media, Melanie was working full-time as a senior vice president of retail development at the Lowell Five Cent Savings Bank. She had been with the bank for thirty-two years, and though she loved her job, it could be quite stressful. She was also dealing with medical issues within her family. Her husband, Alan (Al), has suffered from Crohn's disease since he was a teenager and undergone many surgeries over the years. According to Mayo Clinic, "Crohn's disease is an inflammatory bowel disease (IBD)."[9] Crohn's disease results in

9 "Crohn's Disease," Mayo Clinic, accessed April 4, 2020.

symptoms of abdominal pain, diarrhea, weight loss, and malnutrition due to the inflammation within the digestive tract. Not everyone who has Crohn's disease is affected the same way, but the disease is debilitating, often making it difficult for people to work and manage their life.[10]

Crohn's disease has no cure, but treatments exist that can reduce inflammation and allow an individual to experience remission. Fortunately, Alan had been placed on an anti-inflammatory medicine, Humera, and had been doing very well for about ten years. During this time, he was able to open a local music store in their hometown. Their sons, Alex and Christopher, and future daughter-in-law, Allyssa, helped by working at the store. The music store was a central part of their lives and the community. It was important to Melanie's family that they keep the business moving forward.

Then, in December of 2013, Al was diagnosed with colon cancer. As you can imagine, his diagnosis began a challenging time for Melanie and her family. Her husband was worried he would have to close the music store, but their sons and Allyssa worked hard to keep it open. Alex was a musician and gave lessons at the store, and the whole community rallied behind the family. The store had allowed them to build relationships with the public over the years, and those same people wanted to support him in whatever way possible. You may know a similar story of a community that comes together to support a family undergoing a difficult time. We see these stories in the news and especially on social media today.

10 "Crohn's Disease"

In April 2014, Al underwent surgery for colon cancer. Melanie stayed home to care for him. Melanie writes, "In May of 2014, he was able to come home, but it was discovered after the surgery his lack of energy was due to his intestines' inability to absorb vitamins from food. He was placed on what they call TPN, total parenteral nutrition, which is a supplement that he received every night. These supplements are hooked up through an IV, and when he got home from the hospital, I became his pseudo nurse. I was the one that would prepare these nighttime IV bags so that he would be able to rest. These IV treatments are something he will have to do for the rest of his life. So, we were settling into our new normal of life." Melanie returned to work in June 2014 while still taking care of Al and setting up his IV bags every night.

Melanie's life had been focused on Alan and his health for more than a decade. I know from my own experience of caring for a terminally ill spouse that everything you do and every decision you make is dependent on how well they are doing at that particular time. Setting aside your own feelings, aches, and pains is easy when you are caring for another. Melanie had spent years doing this, always taking care of her husband and family.

I asked Melanie if she knew about the ALS Ice Bucket Challenge that summer, and she replied. "I remember being home in probably July of 2014, for some reason, and I remember seeing on the *Today Show*, I believe, something about the Ice Bucket Challenge. It was a segment where one of the newscasters was challenged by someone to pour a bucket of ice water over their head. I remember thinking, *Well, that's interesting. I've never heard of that before.* Then, as the summer went on, it was everywhere. There were sports figures, entertainment people, political people…just any group that you can imagine was taking this challenge. It was all over social media posts on Facebook. There were news reports every day of a new group taking the challenge, and they started to explain the origination was the ALS Ice Bucket Challenge. I knew that it had to do with some young men who had been diagnosed with ALS at very young ages.

"Now, I knew what Lou Gehrig's disease was, or I'd heard of it. I can't say that I totally knew back then what it meant or what the life expectancy was. I just knew that it was a horrible disease that had been around since the 1920s. It had been brought to light in the 1940s when Lou Gehrig was diagnosed, as he was dying and had to leave baseball."

"One of the things I remember about the ALS Ice Bucket Challenge was a friend of mine, Tina, was on Facebook in her backyard, and she had been challenged by one of her friends, and then she was challenging others. As she poured the bucket over her head I thought, *Huh, no one's challenged me,* which I thought was interesting. I was a little insulted! When I think back now to what was going on in our lives, with my husband's diagnosis and his surgery and new things we had to do to keep him healthy, I now understand why I wasn't challenged. I had enough challenges going on myself, but I did pay attention to it when it was on TV or Facebook, or people were talking about it."

Pete Frates and Pat Quinn, both diagnosed with ALS, and others, were at the root of the ALS Ice Bucket Challenge. They started the chain reaction of posting and sharing videos of people taking the challenge and asking them to support ALS. In this way, the ALS Ice Bucket Challenge quickly went viral, with many people taking the opportunity to make their own video and post it to social media. And the fact that the challenge was taking place during the summer probably didn't hurt its success! The challenge might not have gotten the attention it deserved if it had happened in January.

Melanie said, "I recall an interview that I saw with Pete's mother, Nancy, and she spoke of how dedicated Pete was to this cause. And it wasn't for him, because he knew that whatever he did was probably not going to benefit him, due to how long it takes to get results when you're raising money for cures or treatments. Pete was determined to fight ALS, which was a disease that no one had paid much attention to and there was very little treatment. There was one treatment that had been developed, I believe in the '70s, but it didn't have much promise. I believe they were developing a new treatment. I found out later that due to the money raised by the ALS Ice Bucket Challenge, the treatment got pushed through all the channels that it needed to go through a little faster. It was quite something to watch this ALS Ice Bucket Challenge develop and grow."

You'll learn more about Melanie's story throughout the book as we follow her journey through symptoms, diagnosis, and living with ALS. I hope you will find it helps you connect with the importance of nonprofits and better understand why nonprofits' effective use of social media to raise awareness and educate the public is imperative.

I want to leave this chapter with words from Pete Frates. They show his mindset on the importance of educating people about ALS through social media while continuing to fight for a cure. His vision is what is making a difference in the lives of those with ALS today. Frates said, "The thing I always tell people is to Google three little letters, ALS. Learn how much it can devastate the mind, body, and soul. Frankly, it's just awful, but there is hope because of the Ice Bucket Challenge. So I thank you for the continued support. Let's strike out ALS. Sincerely, Uncle Pete"[11]

---

11 Pete Frates, "New Book Reveals the Inspiring Story Behind the Ice Bucket Challenge," TODAY, November 3, 2017, video 5:22.

CHAPTER 2

A BRIEF HISTORY OF NONPROFITS

Have you ever wondered why nonprofits exist? The United States has quite a different perspective on nonprofit organizations compared to many other countries. Our roots in the United States and the development of our country play a big role in how we view citizenship and the well-being of our populace. The United States has a long history, though a relatively young one compared to that of other countries, of how we take care of others. The nation was formed with a "can-do" spirit that influences how we think about taking care of people. In many other parts of the world, where socialism and communism prevail, the government is seen as the one who should take care of the people. In the United States, based on our democratic form of government, our pursuit of independence has driven the need for individuals to care for those who cannot care for themselves. This lack of federal care continues to evolve today, in part due to the controlling party of the government at a given time. Other countries do care for people; the difference is who is responsible, the government or the private sector.

This unique approach in the United States has resulted in the formation of volunteer groups and nonprofits that are built to solve some of society's problems. Not all would agree that this is the way it should be, but from the American perspective, this is how the nonprofit sector functions. Nonprofits fill the gaps between government and society. Citizens can identify a need and then put a plan in action to solve the problem.

LAYING THE GROUNDWORK

There are some things that are helpful to know before we get too far into the book. A nonprofit is a special type of business designated by the Internal Revenue Service (IRS) as a 501(c)(3), a charitable business. A nonprofit has a mission statement it is expected to carry out, and an organization measures itself not just by financial means, but by whether or not it is fulfilling its mission. There are no owners of the business, and any profit made is turned back into the organization to help it grow its programs and services. The nonprofit does not pay any taxes on its business or property. In fact, the government sees its contribution to the nonprofit as being the equivalent of those lost revenues.

Suppose you donate one hundred dollars to a nonprofit. You take a tax deduction for one hundred dollars. If you are in the 28 percent tax bracket, you don't have to pay twenty-eight dollars to the government. In turn, the government considers that twenty-eight dollars *its* support of the nonprofit.

There are many different types of nonprofits, including those centered on education, human service, health, culture, religion, science, literacy, safety, and prevention of cruelty to children or animals. There are other categories within the 501(c) designation, but for this book, I will look at only 501(c)(3) organizations. Examples of 501(c)(3)s are the American Red Cross, Boys & Girls Clubs of America, Habitat for Humanity, New Hampshire Humane Society, and small local nonprofits like food pantries and environmental and wildlife preservation groups.

Nonprofits impact our lives every day, and just the sheer number of existing nonprofits is startling. According to Statista, approximately 1.54 million nonprofits were registered with the IRS in 2016, an increase from 1.48 million in 2006.[12] In addition, the Urban Institute's National Center for Charitable Statistics found the nonprofit sector contributed an estimated "$985.4 billion to the US economy in 2015, composing 5.4 percent of the country's gross domestic product (GDP)."[13]

Nonprofits have a huge impact on the economy in terms of employment and services. Many people are unaware of just how important this sector is for jobs and income. The Johns Hopkins Center for Civil Society Studies' 2019 Nonprofit Employment Report states, "Economists regularly consider

---

12 Erin Duffin, "Revenues of reporting nonprofit organizations in the U.S. from 1998 to 2016," Statista.com, August 30, 2016, accessed September 6, 2020.

13 Brice McKeever, "The Nonprofit Sector in Brief 2018: Public Charities, Giving and Volunteering," Urban Institute: National Center for Charitable Statistics, accessed February 5, 2020.

any industry or economic sector that employs 5% of a country's workforce to be a 'major' industry or sector. It is therefore notable that the 12.3 million paid workers employed by US nonprofit establishments as of 2016 accounted for a substantial 10.2% of the total US private workforce."[14] As you can see, nonprofits' services have a huge effect on our citizens.

CHARITY & PHILANTHROPY DEFINED: WHY THEY MATTER

I am providing a definition of two words commonly used in the nonprofit sector: *charity* and *philanthropy*. Knowing this is important, in part because of how we think about the effect of nonprofits, but also because confusing the two is easy if you don't have a clear understanding.

Charity is defined by author and nonprofit expert Michael J. Worth as "giving intended to meet current individual human needs or to alleviate suffering."[15] Examples include giving to disaster relief, disability causes, food programs, and humane societies. Often, an emotional element causes people to give. They may know someone affected by the problem or feel spurred to give based on news coverage of an event. When you make a donation like this, you expect the people who are suffering will benefit immediately from your help. Charity is what drove people to become involved in the ALS Ice Bucket Challenge. Once they saw and understood the problem, they

---

14 Lester M. Salamon Chelsea L. Newhouse & S. Wojciech Sokolowski, "The 2018 Nonprofit Employment Report." accessed February 8, 2020.

15 Michael Worth, *Nonprofit Management: Principles and Practice*, (Los Angeles: SAGE Publication, Inc., 2014), 20.

wanted to help, even though that meant dumping a bucket of icy water over their heads!

Philanthropy is an investment in the long-term solution to a problem. Donors know finding a solution to the problem or making an improvement in society requires a much larger sum and that the problem cannot be solved quickly, though it can be improved.[16] Examples include the building of a new cancer center, an endowed scholarship fund, providing clean water for all, or a new research facility to develop cures for diseases. A basic understanding of charity and philanthropy will help you better understand the history behind nonprofits and how we have arrived at where we are today. Both played a role in the development and growth of nonprofits in the United States.

The concept of nonprofits originated in ancient times when the Greeks and Romans viewed citizenry, community, and social responsibility as necessary parts of society. This view persisted in cultures and traditional religious sects in which the idea of helping others was a desirable characteristic to be emulated by followers.[17]

In 1601, English law adopted a Statute of Charitable Uses and the Poor Law. They were approved partly to recognize the difference between church and government, in this case, the Church of England and the British government, and to define what types of activities were to be undertaken by charities.[18]

---

16 Worth, *Nonprofit Management*, 20.

17 Worth, *Nonprofit Management*, 19.

18 Ibid.

As immigrants came to the United States, this foundation is what guided the very earliest attempts at forming organizations to help people. I do not intend to imply that these attempts came easily to citizens. As religion played such a large role in their lives, the line between church and state created challenges.

In 1835, Alexis de Tocqueville wrote *Democracy in America*, as he was quite taken with the differences between Americans and Europeans. In his introduction, he notes the vast contrast between people who have a long history with a class system based on birth and those who have gone to the United States with the opportunity to be limited only by their own talents. He observed that the latter were able to form voluntary groups of citizens to take up a cause, including public safety, industry, and morality.[19]

Tocqueville was struck by how the citizens of the United States approached solving societal problems. "As soon as several of the inhabitants of the United States have taken up an opinion or a feeling which they wish to promote to the world they look out for mutual assistance."[20] We should note that this involvement was sometimes seen as a way to control people and their actions. Religion still played an active role in society, and many followers used it to rein in activities that went against their religious beliefs. David Hammack, author and historian, states, "In the United States associations are

---

19 Aleksandra Pruszewicz and Angela Vander Hulst, "Key Dates and Events in American Philanthropic History 1815 to Present," Learning to Give, accessed April 23, 2020.

20 David C. Hammack, ed., *Making the Nonprofit Sector in the United States: a Reader*, (Bloomington: Indiana University Press), 152.

established to promote the public safety, commerce, industry, morality, and religion."[21] These organizations were the first to address societal issues in the United States that the government did not always address. In Europe, aristocrats took on this role, so involvement was very top-down, whereas in the United States the problems were addressed by the people, who wanted to be able to make decisions by themselves.

This early history laid the groundwork for the development of civil and civic-minded society and was instrumental in the formation of nonprofit organizations.

Well, you might say, this is all very interesting, but how did we get to the nonprofit sector we know now? This is a very good question.

UNITED STATES HISTORY AND ITS ROLE

You might be surprised to learn that World War II brought about an interest in nonprofits. Some of your grandparents may remember what it was like to live through the experience and the years following. As the United States entered the war, the need to raise funds and conserve resources became important. Everyone in the country was called on to provide help, and whether by growing victory gardens, saving tin foil for scrap, making bandages, or knitting garments to keep soldiers warm, few communities were not impacted by the efforts. Americans began to see that by volunteering and fundraising, they could join with other organizations to help with the war effort. For example, the American Red

---

21 Hammack, *Making the Nonprofit Sector in the United States*, 143.

Cross started the first blood donation program, and volunteers helped with the Salvation Army and the YMCA. People began to see that by working with other nonprofit organizations, they were better able to help others, reduce costs, and leverage available resources.[22]

If you want to learn more about what happened in the period following World War II, I encourage you to read Robert Putnam's book *Bowling Alone: The Collapse and Revival of American Community.*[23] While not specifically writing about nonprofits, Putnam offers a unique view of the transformation of small-town America and the growth of cities. People of this era put a real emphasis on community and civic engagement, and Putnam examines this time through a variety of lenses that will give you a better understanding of life at that time and how behaviors have changed.

To give you one example, before the 1950s, front porches were welcome places to meet and talk with your neighbors and passersby. Thus, communities had stronger social connections. When television became available and popular, more families stayed inside their homes instead of utilizing their porches. Over time, this contributed to a disconnect with neighborhood society. If you don't feel connected to your neighbors, developing empathy for them and other struggles that affect society is more challenging.[24]

---

22 Hana Muslic, "A Brief History of Nonprofit Organizations (And What We Can Learn)," *Nonprofit Hub*, Oct 27, 2017.

23 Robert J. Putnam, *Bowling Alone: The Collapse and Revival of American Community*, (New York: Simon & Schuster, 2000).

24 Ibid.

The nonprofit sector was not recognized or defined until the 1975 report "Giving in America."[25] According to Michael Worth, "The Filer Commission report came at a time when the nonprofit sector was expanding, in part reflecting changes in government policy. The 1960s and early 1970s were a period of increasing government spending on social programs, starting with the Great Society programs of President Lyndon Johnson. In many cases, government funds were channeled to nonprofit organizations, which provided the actual services."[26] During this time, nonprofits had opportunities to establish themselves and provide services to those in need.

In the 1980s, federal funding for nonprofits changed. There was increased political pressure to provide reduced funding, so nonprofits no longer received government funding to the previous extent. This change had an impact on nonprofits, including higher education. Students and their families were asked to take on a more significant portion of the cost of higher education with the addition of parent loans and unsubsidized student loans.

Changes in higher education funding continued, though. In correspondence with Teresa Jardon, senior associate director of financial aid at UMass Lowell, she wrote, "For many years, from the space race until the 1980s, higher education was seen as a public benefit for the common good (the more educated

---

25 Report of the Commission on Private Philanthropy and Public Needs, "*Giving in America: Toward a Stronger Voluntary Sector,*" December 31, 1974.

26 Michael J. Worth, *Nonprofit Management: Principles & Practices*, (Thousand Oaks: Sage Publications, 2012), 21.

the workforce, the more productive they would be). There was tremendous public support behind funding public education. Federal and state governments provided significant funding toward institutions as well as directly to students. In the 1980s & into the 1990s, perceptions shifted. Public perception included that direct payments to individuals were wrought with fraud. Tax credits were provided to those with incomes high enough to benefit from a credit (those who owe taxes) while direct funding to students dropped when adjusted for inflation. In more recent years, perceptions have shifted again—higher education is commonly viewed as an individual benefit—one those individuals should pay for themselves—rather than a societal benefit for the common good."[27] Public perception of public good versus private good and who benefits still impacts society today.

WHERE WE ARE TODAY

While the changes may have some benefit, they have also created issues for nonprofits. Nonprofits that have never had to market themselves before find they need to learn to manage and market their organization as if it were a for-profit business, often with considerably less expertise and funding available. This challenge is particularly true of smaller nonprofits, for which managing government contracts and developing and implementing marketing programs can be difficult due to limited staff and funding.

The development of the internet changed the way businesses and nonprofits operate. Prior to the ALS Ice Bucket Challenge,

27 Teresa Jardon, email message to author, July 10, 2020.

larger nonprofits were already utilizing social media as part of their marketing strategy. They understood social media could help them, even if they didn't completely understand how. It was a learning curve for them, too! In an interview, Colleen Gordon, social media marketer, reflected, "In 2008-2009, as the economy was taking a dive, I had an opportunity to work for a company and build their social media. My job was to grow the businesses' social media presence, along with other responsibilities. I could see it getting really big, because Facebook was transforming from being a college platform at the time. Business pages were just becoming a concept; I got to build out everything. I had a say in creating the strategy and getting the message out to the public."[28]

Changes in demographics affect who donates. Millennials, long ignored as potential donors, are now between the ages of twenty-five and forty and are about to enter some prime giving years. Diane Orson said, "In fact, while on average about 70 percent of Americans donate, millennials give at rate of about 85 percent."[29] Millennials are a very social media savvy demographic, all the more reason why refining social media marketing will benefit nonprofit organizations.

Now that you have some background information about nonprofits, we can move forward to best determine how to use social media to raise awareness and educate the public. It's time to learn and embrace the way we can showcase smaller nonprofits and what they do. This is our future!

---

28 Colleen Gordon (who working with a student health digital publication at the time) in discussion with the author.

29 Diane Orson, "Millennials And Charitable Giving: A New Approach To Philanthropy," National Public Radio, December 27, 2019.

CHAPTER 3

THE ROLE OF PHILANTHROPY

Who do you think of when you hear the word "philanthropy"? Maybe you would say Bill and Melinda Gates, who created the largest foundation in the world. Perhaps you think of Warren Buffet, an American businessman widely considered to be the most successful investor of the twentieth century. You would be right! Were they the first? No, but they are certainly some of the most prominent philanthropists of the twentieth century. But don't mistake philanthropists as only wealthy people; if we only relied on wealth as a criterion, we would miss a significant number of philanthropists. They include those who also use their knowledge and expertise to address the root causes of significant problems.

You might be wondering why I am including philanthropy as part of the story of how the ALS Ice Bucket Challenge changed the way smaller nonprofits had to think about using social media. After all, the money given during the challenge would be classified as charitable rather than philanthropic.

Most donations were from individuals contributing amounts of one hundred dollars. The reason I include it here is because if it weren't for philanthropy, there would be little money available for ALS research and treatment at clinics and hospitals. Philanthropy requires taking a bird's-eye view of the problem, looking at what is being done currently, and recognizing that solving a problem like ALS is going to take expanded collaboration, study, and research. Philanthropy requires much more funding than is available through charitable donations. While the ALS Ice Bucket Challenge brought awareness and funds, it accomplished only a small bit of what needs to be done to develop a cure.

Let's learn more about how philanthropy came to play a significant role in nonprofits and societal change.

INTRODUCING ANDREW CARNEGIE

In the late 1800s and early 1900s, several Americans built successful businesses and accrued great wealth. Andrew Carnegie was an early philanthropist, giving during his lifetime. However, only in his later life did he begin to put a plan into action that would leave a lasting impact on the United States. In a true rags-to-riches tale, he worked hard and advanced himself, making money from oil, railroads, and steel. Even at a young age, he believed in using his money to help others. Carnegie said, "I propose to take an income no greater than $50,000 per annum! Beyond this I need ever earn, make no effort to increase my fortune, but spend the surplus each year for benevolent purposes!"[30] In this way, Carnegie was able to lay the groundwork for his contribution to improving the lives of others.

Since this is a book, and I have a lifelong interest in books and libraries, I think it is important to know Carnegie is the reason we have the public libraries of today. When Carnegie was growing up, there were no public libraries. A few wealthy people had libraries, but they were not accessible to the public. As a young boy, Carnegie was introduced to books by an uncle, and this influenced his decision later in life to use his wealth to build public libraries.[31] Carnegie donated money to build libraries, as he believed everyone should have access to books, not just the wealthy. According to Kriston Capps, "Between 1893 and 1919—a three-decade run that librarians refer to as the Golden Age of the American public library system—Carnegie paid to build 1,689 libraries in the US. These seeded the DNA for nearly every American library built before the end of World War II."[32] Carnegie donated the funds to build and provide the books for the library but required that the city or town provide the land, operation, and maintenance.

Today, Carnegie libraries still exist, and Carnegie laid the foundation for continuing generations to use and benefit from public libraries. Think of Carnegie every time you read a book!

---

30 "Andrew Carnegie Becomes a Capitalist, 1856," 2007, EyeWitness to History.

31 *Andrew Carnegie Biography.* Biography.com Editors, June 24, 2019.

32 Kriston Capps, "How Andrew Carnegie Built the Architecture of American Literacy," *Bloomberg CityLab*, October 28, 2014.

In 1889, Carnegie wrote *The Gospel of Wealth*, which started as a series of articles, and said that the wealthy had an obligation to use their money to improve society and the lives of others, as that wealth was incurred by the society that helped them gain their wealth. Carnegie stated, "This, then, is held to be the duty of the man of Wealth: First, to set an example of modest, unostentatious living, shunning display or extravagance; to provide moderately for the legitimate wants of those dependent upon him; and after doing so to consider all surplus revenues which come to him simply as trust funds, which he is called upon to administer, and strictly bound as a matter of duty to administer in the manner which, in his judgment, is best calculated to produce the most beneficial results for the community...."[33] Carnegie was not the only one to lead this cause, which included John D. Rockefeller, Henry Ford, and John Paul Getty, but he was recognized as a pioneer in philanthropy. Their philanthropic efforts were possible because they had made their money through investments in steel, oil, cars, and railroads. This success allowed Carnegie and others to lay the groundwork for philanthropy as we know it today.

FOUNDATION ESTABLISHMENT: HOW PAST PHILANTHROPISTS AFFECT US TODAY

I included this information about Carnegie because I believe it is a fascinating glimpse into a period of history that affects nonprofit organizations today. His work has resulted in others' taking up his charge, including Bill and Melinda Gates with the Bill & Melinda Gates Foundation, Warren

---

33 Andrew Carnegie, 1889, *The Gospel of Wealth*, 12.

Buffett with the Buffett Foundation, Oprah Winfrey with the Oprah Winfrey Charitable Foundation, and J.K. Rowling with the Lumos Foundation. Family foundations are typically endowed by the family and meant to last in perpetuity. Their mission is to provide funding to causes they care about in ways that can continue after they are gone.

In addition to individuals and families establishing charitable foundations, many corporations and communities have also done so. Establishing a corporate or private foundation allows a company to move funds to the foundation in a tax beneficial manner. In addition, a foundation also streamlines the process of granting charitable requests, as there is a vetting process for grant applicants that allows the foundation to fund requests that align with their mission.

Community foundations are usually established in cities and towns to manage donated funds from individuals, families, or public entities. For example, multiple endowed scholarships for a high school provide giving opportunities for those without enough money to fund their own foundation. Community foundations are also a way to manage smaller investment funds of a local nonprofit. A foundation can manage many separate funds and cost-effectively provide these services. Because the endowed investments are pooled, the cost of managing them is much less than if each fund had to pay investment fees.

TAX DEDUCTIBLE!

I would be remiss if I didn't mention the history of donations to a 501(c)(3) nonprofit being tax-deductible for the donor.

In 1917, Congress established the War Revenue Act, which permitted individuals to receive a tax deduction for donations made to a charitable organization. Congress felt this would encourage charitable donations, in part due to rising income taxes needed to fund World War I. The following year, this was extended to include charitable bequests on estate tax returns. After another eighteen years, corporations were able to file a tax deduction for charitable donations on their corporate tax returns.[34]

Recent tax changes in 2017 impacted standard deductions. The amount of the standard deduction increased, but it eliminated the ability to deduct charitable contributions unless the individual qualifies to itemize their deductions. If an individual has deductions that exceed the standard deduction, then they can itemize charitable deductions, but this option is only available for individuals and families with a larger income. This change caused a great deal of concern for nonprofits, as they feared they would lose donations from those who used to give between $25 and $99 each year.

Though the donations were smaller, there were more of them. People who supported a nonprofit in the past could no longer deduct their donation. In 2019, Greg Rosalsky found that "[the] fall in itemization contributed to a massive fall in people who claim the charitable deduction. Overall, in 2018, despite a strong economy, American households reduced their charitable giving by over $15 billion, the largest decline

---

34 Arnsberger, Paul, Melissa Ludlum, Margaret Riley, & Mark Stanton. 2008 *A History of the Tax-Exempt Sector:* An SOI Perspective. Accessed April 26, 2020.

since the Great Recession. It seems clear the change in the tax code reduced the incentive to give for many taxpayers."[35]

Perhaps in recognition of this decline, changes to the tax law are forthcoming. According to Certified Public Accountant Tawnya Finkel, a change for those choosing the standard deduction is expected in 2020 that will allow deductions up to $300 of charitable cash contributions. This will hopefully encourage the millions of people who had supplied nonprofits with smaller donations in the past to consider making donations, and in doing so express their support of organizations and their missions.

Many nonprofits rely on donations to provide services to meet their mission. In addition, nonprofits can use those donations that are not specific in their designated purpose for overhead expenses, something not typically covered by funding grants. These donations provide a way for the nonprofit to "keep the lights on," something smaller nonprofits often struggle with in terms of operating expenses.

It is hoped philanthropy and charitable giving continue to grow and play a major role in nonprofits by providing funding for organizations that would struggle to provide services without the support of individuals, corporations, and foundations but also by addressing problems that affect society.

---

35 Greg Rosalsky, "Charitable Giving Is Down. It Might Be Time To Reform The Charitable Deduction," *Planet Money*, November 12, 2019.

WHY PHILANTHROPY MATTERS

Many of us have received the benefits of philanthropy and haven't even realized it. If you are a student and received a scholarship, attended a professional live theater production, or visited a museum, this likely happened because of philanthropy. In his book *Why Philanthropy Matters: How the Wealthy Give, and What It Means for Our Economic Well-Being*, Zoltan Acs explained that philanthropy is important to our society as an economic good and a moral good. It is both a way to encourage investments from others and an investment in the future.[36] Given a strong focus, philanthropy can provide a vehicle for change through innovation and research, such as what is needed to find a cure for ALS.

Hospitals and research facilities rely on large-scale philanthropic donations to help fund their missions. Philanthropic donations are often how hospitals expand, by building new wings dedicated to a specific type of care, and how researchers fund their facilities and research costs to discover treatment and cures for diseases. You've probably seen the name of an individual on the side of a hospital building or new expansion, like the Norris Cotton Cancer Center or the Curt and Shonda Schilling ALS Clinic at Lahey Hospital and Medical Center. These facilities were made possible through generous philanthropic donations from individuals and foundations.

Keeping this in mind, let's return to Melanie's story and hear what was happening in her life before she was diagnosed with ALS.

---

36 Zoltan J. Acs, *Why Philanthropy Matters: How the Wealthy Give, and What It Means for Our Economic Well-Being* (Princeton, New Jersey: Princeton University Press, 2013).

THE ROAD TO ALS DISCOVERY: MELANIE'S HUSBAND CONTINUES TO BATTLE COLON CANCER

In this next part of the story, Melanie's awareness and discovery of her symptoms of ALS provided an understanding of what was happening in her life pre-diagnosis. This story shows the time before her diagnosis when Melanie had to put her husband and his medical needs first. From my own experience, I know how caring for someone with cancer can take over your whole life, sometimes ignoring issues you may be having because they seem minor in terms of what the other person is going through.

Melanie said, "In 2014 to 2015, the doctors attempted to give my husband, Alan, a round of chemotherapy to ensure that the cancer would not return. This proved to be impossible, because his body was so weak at the time that the chemo just made him sicker. In the end, he never got the chemo; it was decided that the risk was too high. In addition to this health issue, he was now very prone to infections, due to the line that he needed to receive TPN (Total Parenteral Nutrition) at night; this resulted in frequent infections."

From 2015 to 2016, Melanie's husband had multiple infections in his line that would require hospitalization. It became a cycle of emergency room visits, hospitalization, and home, only to have the process start all over again. Melanie said, "On a few occasions, the infection would come on so quickly that his fever would spike. He always resisted going to the hospital, because he had spent so much time there, that we might have waited a little too long to go in. There were a couple of infections when his fever was up to 103 in no time, so I would have to call an ambulance."

At the time, Melanie and her family were living in Pepperell, Massachusetts, a twenty to twenty-five mile ride to Lahey Clinic in Burlington, Massachusetts. This is where all of his doctors were and where they put in and maintained his TPN line. Melanie said, "When his fever would spike, I would be very nervous about driving him the twenty miles, so I had to call an ambulance. The ambulance personnel, because of his condition, refused to take him that far. We had to go to Southern New Hampshire Medical, a thirteen-mile drive. They did their best there, but they didn't deal with these kinds of intravenous lines. There was really nothing they could do; sometime in the next day, they would get an ambulance to take him to Lahey when he was stable. It came to the point where Lahey Clinic would say, you know, 'The best thing to do is bring him directly here.' This means I became the ambulance driver; when his fever would spike and he would be sick, I would get him into our car. We had a Ford Explorer at the time, and sometimes it was like an ambulance because he'd lay down in the back, and I would drive him to Lahey Clinic. This usually happened in the middle of the night, rarely was it during the day, but there were so many infections that it was at all different times of the day."

Melanie and Alan were fortunate to have good friends and neighbors. "On one occasion, I did call my neighbor, a good friend of mine, and she came over and helped me get him in the car because that is difficult when someone has 103 temperature. I think this time the fever might have been 104, and he was very incoherent and not able to reason. He was even a little delirious, so getting him to the car was a challenge for me. Our bedroom was on the third floor, so that meant taking him down two flights of stairs and then down the front porch steps to the driveway. My neighbor came with me to the hospital, and stayed with me until probably three o'clock in the morning. They couldn't remove the line; he needed the line to live. This often resulted in a minimum seven-day hospital stay."

At this point, Melanie and her husband realized it made sense for them to move closer to Lahey Clinic to reduce the travel time and distance. Living closer would also enable an ambulance to take him directly to Lahey Clinic. "In 2015, we bought a house in Chelmsford and moved in. It wasn't long after that when he had more infections, and they did take him to Lahey Clinic. This was a much safer situation for everyone."

This was an extremely busy and stressful time for Melanie. Her husband was her number one concern, and as many caregivers do, she wasn't thinking about her own health. Once there was a reduction in the number of hospitalizations for Al, life returned to a more normal pace, though always with concerns for his health. Melanie said, "As all this was going on, I started to realize that I had tingling feelings in my hands and arms. A few years before this, I went to a therapeutic massage professional, and I would tell her about it. It wasn't anything I mentioned to my doctors, but there wasn't really anything they could do. They started giving me B12 because my level of B12 was low. It would come and go, and it was just more of an annoyance than anything else."

As you can see, Melanie faced many challenges in her personal life as a caregiver to her husband. Now she had to address her own symptoms and health. You'll learn more about Melanie's story in the coming chapters.

CHAPTER 4

THE ADVENT OF SOCIAL MEDIA: WHAT MAKES IT SO POWERFUL

How is it that something that did not even exist twenty-five years ago has such a major impact on our lives today? Think about it! Social media has changed our lives and how we connect with others. It affects our family, our friendships, our work relationships, and how we make decisions on what to buy or not buy. There is very little that we do today that is not influenced by social media.

Social media is just one part of a marketing strategy, but for many organizations, particularly smaller ones, it may be the only one they use regularly. Yes, nonprofit organizations often have brochures and a website, and keeping these updated is important. However, cost is always a factor, and social media may seem the easiest, most immediate way to deliver a message. Later in the book, I'll describe how this idea fits in with a strategy, but I want to make the point here that having a marketing strategy is critical.

Due to advancements in technology, most people view their social media via phones. Dr. Mark Yim, assistant professor of marketing at UMass Lowell, said, "Mobile is going to be the primary medium where people get marketing messages." Mobile social media presence helps you get noticed, but it is not easy! There is so much "noise," which makes getting people to even slow down as they swipe down their feed challenging. You only have a few seconds to grab attention, and your content must interest them enough to stop scrolling down. Try this yourself. Pull up your phone and check one of your social media accounts. Start scrolling and see how long it takes you to stop. For me, it takes one to three seconds to stop and read what is posted. *Plus*, what makes me stop is related to two things: how well I know and like the person or organization that posted and if it had a catchy title or image. And really, the image is more likely to grab my attention. It must be something relevant to me on that particular day that makes me even think about clicking on a link.

I am also considering how much time I have at that specific moment. I may say I'll go back to a friend's post and look at it later, but it doesn't resonate with me enough to read it now. How many times do I forget to go back and check it out? If you are like me, I frequently forget, though my intentions were good. The post must speak to me now. How do we get there?

VISUAL POWER

Images can be extremely powerful. They are the first thing the eyes see before they read any text, so the image must be strong and able to capture the viewers' attention. I recently had a group of students working on a nonprofit project to make suggestions for improving the nonprofit's social media. The first thing they showed me was how another chapter of the same organization in another state was so clearly using color and images to tie to the nonprofit organization's national branding. The images from the exemplar organization were high-quality and delivered a message with few or no words. Smiling faces, multicultural images of hands coming together, and consistent use of color across all posts helped convey connectedness to the nonprofit.

In comparison, the images used by the local organization the students were helping had too many people in the pictures, making it difficult to clearly see any one of them, and the images did not convey any connection between the participants and the activity. In other words, the picture could have been a random picture of people at any event.

Compare that to the exemplar: The use of color played a role in terms of catching your eye and coordinating with a brand. Where text was used in the post, it was used clearly and concisely on a background color that reduced the noise and let your eyes focus on the words. When viewed side by side, the contrast between how the two organizations used social media was remarkable. The excitement of the students was palpable; they wanted to help their project's organization improve their social media. They could envision posts that would resonate with their audience once they found a way to present a coherent template.

SO, HOW DO WE GET THIS DONE?

Wade Harmon, social media examiner, recommends five ways to improve social media posts. These include the aforementioned use of images and color, but Harmon also discusses *the importance of using words that serve as a call to action.* These should be used to create an emotional connection and a way to engage with the organization. Harmon also suggests using questions as a good way to get the reader to think about what you are asking and how they can help be part of the solution.[37] Questions or polls slow the reader down and offer them the chance to consider how they might respond.

Successful social media marketers know their success is about content—not just supplying any content, but *content that is relevant to your audience* and your goals for the organization. For example, perhaps you want to post an image of clients enjoying an outing. Thinking strategically about why you want to share this image is important. Do you want to inform? Raise awareness of programs? Attract donors? Solicit volunteers? Just posting an image and hoping for the best is not enough! You have to think carefully about the wording of the post, the social media channel you use, and even the best time of the day or week to post this information.

---

37 Wade Harman, "5 Psychology Tips to Improve Your Social Media Posts," *Social Media Examiner*, October 7, 2015.

Using links is also important so people can find more information. There is nothing more frustrating than seeing a post that intrigues you and then having to search for the link to learn more. This has often happened to me. The picture is engaging, but now I must search for where to find more information. Good social media posts will include a link to your website that is easy to find.

Viewers have a chance to hear firsthand how your programs help the people you serve. Video can provide a way to showcase, in a caring and empathetic manner, just how much your organization means to clients, constituents, volunteers, and donors. Seeing and hearing the stories of others result in a greater sense of community and hopefully build a stronger connection between the nonprofit and the individual.

THE POWER OF THE ASK THROUGH STRATEGIC TAGGING

We've all been asked to support a cause, whether by a close personal friend or a friend of a friend. Sometimes we have mixed feelings about it, and other times it just seems like the right thing to do. Social media has changed the way we ask friends. Think about it—what could be easier than tagging people online? This is so much easier than having a conversation about it. Prior to the ALS Ice Bucket Challenge, Facebook didn't even have a donate button available! Today, by tagging someone in a request, we are able to reach more people than ever before.

Angel Brunelle, director of development at Boys & Girls Club of Greater Lowell, said, "I remember seeing a friend of mine that I worked with years and years ago who tagged like a hundred people, and all of a sudden you see all these comments from people that you used to know. It made you feel like, 'I need to get involved in this,' because it had that same effect of reaching people all over the country. We were spread all over the country. Yet it had an impact all over the world, reconnecting each other on social media. There was a call to action involved in it."

Angel's story is similar to my own experience. On Giving Tuesday in 2019, I put up a request on Facebook to raise $500 for the Lowell Association for the Blind and tagged friends I thought might be interested. I kicked the ask off with a $100 donation. I honestly didn't think many people would donate, and I expected I'd end up probably giving another $300 on my own. I was shocked at how many people gave. Friends gave—people I hadn't seen for a couple of years, colleagues from work, others who work with people with disabilities, and even my children! Many people gave because they said they had seen my posts about the Lowell Association for the Blind and wanted to support an organization I'd been involved with for so many years. This was my first experience asking people online, and I wonder why I waited so long. In the end, I raised over $575 from over thirty donations, large and small. I think it was the first time I experienced the power of tagging people on social media on a personal level.

Angel had this to say: "She [her friend] really did a great job of using that social connection to get her message out and to get people involved who normally, had she sent me a message individually, I would have ignored it. Had she just posted it without tagging a bunch of people, it probably would have just gone through their feed and been ignored. She really was smart about the way that she engaged everybody. I was thinking of ignoring the request, and then I saw somebody else I know make a donation. I'm like, I can't let them make a donation and not make a donation myself!"

By tagging friends, you reduce the bystander effect. The bystander effect is what happens when too many people are asked to do something, and they start to think, "I'll let someone else take care of this." Strategic tagging of friends by staff, board members, and volunteers can produce higher awareness and donations for the nonprofit. Small donations matter. You may not have realized how your past posts and involvement in a nonprofit affect people and cause them to want to give.

Goodworld, an organization that helps businesses and nonprofits, noted, "Tagging friends with a donation opens a level of micro-targeting that cannot be bought."[38] It allows you to capture your friends' interest at a level that encourages them to support and learn more about your nonprofit. If you think about how we connect with friends offline, you can see the advantage of being able to tag multiple people at once in a request for support of your organization.

---

38 "Tagging Peer to Peer Giving on Facebook," *Goodworld* (blog), August 18, 2018. Accessed April 5, 2020.

The lesson here is never be afraid to ask for support. It may come to you in ways you never dreamed of before, and it can help you rebuild connections, identify potential future donors, and spread the word about your nonprofit. Encourage administrators, staff, board members, and volunteers to join you, too!

CHAPTER 5

WHY NONPROFITS STRUGGLE WITH SOCIAL MEDIA

Think of social media from a nonprofit's perspective. Why wouldn't you use it? It's virtually free, and you can use it to market your organization. Of course you would choose to use it! Here are some easy definitions for the four groups a nonprofit should consider for their individual marketing needs.

- Clients: People who receive the services the nonprofit provides at no or low cost
  - Ex. Recipients of food from a food pantry, programs for adults and children at a disability nonprofit
- Constituents: People who may purchase a service from the nonprofit
  - Ex. Students at a university, people who rent your facility for a wedding
- Volunteers: People who give their time and skills to help the clients or the organization

    - Almost anyone can become a volunteer, teenagers to retired people
- Donors: People who contribute to your nonprofit with funds or in-kind goods or services
    - Ex. Major gift donor, annual fund contributor, board member, or someone who donates office equipment or materials

Social media keeps your clients, constituents, volunteers, and donors apprised of what you are doing. You can use it to fundraise, thank donors and volunteers, and more—the list goes on and on. So, what is the problem? Why aren't more nonprofits using social media more fully to excite and inform their audiences?

STAFFING, MONEY, TIME, AND EXPERTISE: RESOURCES ARE THE REASON NONPROFITS OFTEN STRUGGLE

Lack of resources is an ongoing problem for many organizations. Few smaller nonprofits can dedicate a staff member to social media alone, which means they often cobble together social media posts when and where they can. There is often no plan in place to promote the organization via social media. It can be overwhelming to the person charged with creating posts for the nonprofit, particularly if they are not familiar or comfortable with social media, or because they lack time due to other responsibilities.

In an interview with Elizabeth Cannon, executive director of the Lowell Association for the Blind, she said, "I remember attending a conference and they said, 'Oh, you should have a full-time staff person spending 25 percent of their time managing your social media, and it was like, 'Oh god, we don't have time for that!'" Nonprofits often struggle due to lack of staffing, which results in very limited available time to increase their social media footprint. In addition, although there are several tools available to help nonprofits organize, schedule, and respond to social media posts, just like any other skill, if you don't use it regularly, your skills can lapse. Social media is sometimes handled by only one person, whether full or part-time. If that person leaves the organization, the employee turnover can result in a loss of continuity in keeping the public informed.

LZ Nunn, executive director of Project LEARN, said in an interview, "When we started, we did very little marketing because it was simply me and a ten-hour-a-week college intern. There was no room for marketing, and I didn't think it was a smart thing to do. At that stage, we had to prove some results with proof of concept. We were hustling to get grants for the schools on various programs, so we didn't even do marketing until probably my second or third year in, when we were able to hire a full-time person. Our marketing manager was very creative and had a sharp eye for detail and creating social media buzz, as well as developing and executing events. Not just any event—the right kind of events that help tell your organization's impact story and engage people so that you have something to share. For a newer organization, it can be a challenge to really tell your story well. For example, you know there's a passionate person involved with the organization, and the story has to have just enough fun and whimsy, too. I think that's what's magical about it, and that's what really caught on. It probably captured people's imaginations."

These two executive directors confirm the lack of time and staff in smaller nonprofits to properly utilize social media for marketing. It is easy to understand, and other items often take priority over expending time and effort on social media. Rick Blain, a certified fundraising executive and CEO of nonprofit consulting firm Richard R. Blain & Associates, said, "What I've seen is that with the small nonprofits, they get all excited about doing more with social media, and one of the problems that I've seen is that they lack context, if you will. In other words, they don't recognize that social media is just one piece of their public relations, marketing, and fundraising program. It has to be coordinated with a number of other things. That's the context that I'm talking about."

I also hear, over and over, from smaller nonprofit directors that social media often gets assigned to the youngest person in the organization. They assume that since they use social media in their own lives, they can do it for the nonprofit, too. This is a critical mistake. *Managing your personal social media is quite different than managing social media for a business—for profit or nonprofit!* Choosing the right person to manage social media is so important! Not everyone has the skills needed to do it well.

Rick Blain gave an example of a nonprofit social service agency. "They've asked us to do an evaluation of what they're currently doing with social media—tell them what we think are some strengths and weaknesses, pluses and minuses, and then help them to develop a strategy for expanding their social media. We've also been asked to provide some training to a couple of their staff members that have only a very basic knowledge of social media. As we were preparing to do so, my associate said to me, 'You know, I actually am not crazy about some of the social media they're currently doing. Who are they going to train?' They have a staff member who is really good at graphics; he's been doing their social media. They want to further train him. He's very talented; he does some great work, but designing a brochure is really different from designing a Facebook post."

This is a great example: don't make the mistake of assigning social media to the wrong person—make sure you provide training and guidance. This can be done in a variety of ways, but I particularly like Julia Campbell's book *How to Build and Mobilize a Social Media Community for Your Nonprofit in 90 Days.*[39] Campbell does an excellent job of laying out the process in practical, readable chapters that guide you along the way.

The ALS Ice Bucket Challenge helped nonprofit organizations realize they need to find a way to better use social media to educate, inform, and engage with their clients, constituents, volunteers, and donors. Recognizing that each public is a market segment whose needs and wants from an organization differ is important. While there is sometimes an overlap between them, for example, in the case of a volunteer who is also a donor, each group is a different demographic and is interested in topics that are not always of interest to all. Without the support of these valuable groups, nonprofits would cease to exist.

---

39 Julia Campbell, *How to Build and Mobilize a Social Media Community for Your Nonprofit in 90 Days*, (Lexington: Bold & Bright Media, 2020).

UTILIZING THE RIGHT PLATFORM FOR YOUR ORGANIZATION

Because each public of the nonprofit has specific needs, nonprofits recognize they cannot all be met on just one social media platform. Angel Brunelle of Boys & Girls Club of Greater Lowell said, "Facebook's not going anywhere for us because our target demographic is there. That's where we're going to tell the stories of the Club. Instagram, we use more for our teens, to get them excited because they are a population we have to recruit. Their parents usually don't choose for them to come to the Club; they choose to come to the Club. We're going to stick with Instagram, but it's evolving a little bit, because we have a few more of our donors on Instagram. Still, that's not the audience—normally teens—where we talk about fundraisers and events that are coming up."

Brunelle went on to share how LinkedIn is becoming a marketing channel for them. "Now it seems like LinkedIn is evolving to be more content-oriented and offers more storyline opportunities. We need to revisit this because we used to just post jobs on LinkedIn, and now we need to provide stories more often."

Deciding how many channels to be involved in and where the most effort should be expended can be challenging. According to Brunelle, "We have a Twitter account, and although we haven't found a lot of attention on it, we say, 'Okay, how are we using Twitter now? Are we going to keep using it? What makes the most sense for us, given our resources—where should we spend our energy?'"

This is a question every nonprofit should ask.

In larger nonprofits, typically with budgets over $1 million, there are often people or departments who handle marketing for the organization, so social media management becomes a more delineated role. Smaller nonprofits often rely on everyone to help with social media, including staff, volunteers, and the executive director, which can result in disjointed messages to the public. Developing goals and a strategy to achieve them will allow everyone to focus on the intentional use of social media.

MARKETING STRATEGY? DO WE EVEN HAVE ONE?

I have found in talking with a variety of smaller nonprofits that everyone thinks they have a marketing strategy, but when you ask them what it is, they sometimes have a hard time articulating exactly what they mean. The first and obvious go-to is "Well, we're on social media." But I have to remind students of this all the time: *Social media alone is not a marketing strategy.* It is a part of a larger overall marketing strategy for the organization.

Many smaller nonprofits don't make—or think they have the time—to develop a marketing strategy. Yes, there are a few obvious things—for example, hosting a fundraising special event. Social media marketing may play a role, but it is only one aspect of marketing the event. Everything you do for the event should be tied to marketing. Key partners? Corporate donors? Event guests? Each of these requires a different marketing approach. Otherwise, it is like putting together a puzzle and getting to the end only to discover that two pieces are missing!

I want to stress that *this doesn't have to be a thirty-page marketing plan that ends up sitting on the shelf, never to be looked at again.* In fact, this may be one of the biggest hurdles smaller nonprofits have to overcome. Rather, it should be a comprehensive look at who are our target markets:

- What do we want them to know?
- How are they getting information from us now?
- How would we like to engage them?
- What kind of stories do we want to tell?

The trick is to put this into an *action plan* to help the organization achieve its goals. I've seen many well-written plans that lack actionable items and a point person to be certain each item created is completed within a defined time frame. Without an action plan, knowing how well the nonprofit is meeting its goals is difficult.

More on this later but introducing it now will help you start to think about the goals you want to achieve with social media.

ENGAGEMENT: WHY DOES IT MATTER?

You must understand that social media is not just about posts, but also about creating conversations that connect your audience with what you are doing to help others and make them feel connected to your nonprofit. Too many times, nonprofits seem to put up a post that might be interesting to read but doesn't encourage engagement. Then there is little follow-through in terms of responding to any comments or likes or encouraging people to share the information with their network.

A study by Dunham+Company and Marketing Support Network in 2015 provided an excellent example of what happens when there is no clear plan for using social media. They opened their study by saying, "Imagine one of your organization's donors walks up to you at a social gathering and says—in front of a crowd of strangers—that they absolutely love the work of your organization and hope others will support it too. How should you respond? Well, you certainly wouldn't turn around and start talking to someone else, or stare into space while everyone stood around feeling awkward. If you did, you'd most likely lose that supporter because your response would be quite offensive."[40] Looking at it from this perspective, you can see why engaging with your supporters in a respectful and timely manner is important. The study also found that only 48 percent of nonprofits respond to questions or comments on Facebook and only 55 percent responded to questions or comments on Twitter.[41]

As you can see from the results of the study, there is room for improvement in responses to nonprofit social media posts. Ideally, one person in the organization would have the responsibility to do this. The reality for smaller nonprofits, however, is that they do not have the necessary staffing capabilities. Is it possible to improve? Of course, but first they must understand why providing timely responses matters.

A best practice and common metric is how quickly the nonprofit responds to a post response. Think of your own

---

40 "*Nonprofit Social Media Scorecard | A National Study Analyzing the Social Media Habits of Nonprofits*," Marketing Support Network (2015), accessed May 7, 2020.

41 Ibid.

expectations for a response to a text or chat. For example, I often query my students about what is an adequate response time to a message from a teammate in class. Is it immediately, one hour, eight hours, or twenty-four hours? When you ask a group of students this question, you will get very different answers! Some may think an immediate response should be sent, while others think a day or two is fine. If the team doesn't agree to a specific time for a response, there can be a breakdown in communication. We've all been there. We send a question to someone and are waiting for a quick response, but then it slips down in their messages and gets forgotten. This delay increases frustration and the ability of the team to function well. The same can be said of nonprofit social media responses: they need to be timely and relevant.

The study by Dunham+Company and Marketing Support Network also found that most nonprofits had a very slow response time to donors, a group you would expect to receive a very timely response! Over half the nonprofits in the study responded in forty-eight to seventy-two hours to a donation on Twitter, and 48 percent took that long to respond on Facebook![42] This seems particularly egregious, as nonprofits rely on donors to support the ongoing programs and services of the organization.

WHY RECOGNIZE SHARING?

Perhaps the most valuable asset a nonprofit has is its network of contacts. Sadly, this network is often a very underutilized and misunderstood marketing and social media tool. The

42 Ibid.

people connected to you already have a vested interest in your organization, but each of these individuals also have a tremendous network and community of their own. Encouraging them to share the nonprofit's content and recognizing them when they do are easy and affordable ways to increase awareness of the nonprofit. Rick Blain likes to say, "'People give to people, for people.' The comment people give to people, not to organizations, is often said in my profession. I've added to this because truly, people give to the people who are asking, and they do so for the people who will benefit."

Think about this! When was the last time you were asked to donate by someone in person? Was it to contribute to a specific cause? What made you say yes or no? It is quite likely you said yes because you knew the person, you knew the cause they asked you to support was important to them, and saying no to a personal ask from a friend or even an acquaintance is harder than saying no to a stranger.

Asking a friend to share a social media post has all of the same characteristics as asking for a donation. In fact, it might even be less risky because you aren't asking the friend to spend money, just a share to spread the word. Your friend likely knows how much you care about the organization, too. Sharing social media posts is so powerful. You are not asking someone to give up much, but you are asking them to make a small effort to help improve the lives of others.

To summarize, nonprofits are failing at social media because they are often understaffed and overworked, they don't understand how social media plays a role in marketing the organization, and they don't take advantage of their existing network of clients, constituents, volunteers, and donors to help promote the organization through social media. Luckily, this can all be fixed once an understanding of its importance is conveyed to people who can help the nonprofit make a difference. It's up to *you* to make sure you are letting your audience know how they can help and why it is so important.

While the ALS Ice Bucket Challenge was truly a social media and fundraising success, there are still people being diagnosed with ALS every day. Funding and research are needed, as there is still no cure. The ALS Association (ALSA) continues to raise money, though it has never been able to repeat the tremendous financial success of the 2014 ALS Ice Bucket Challenge.

Below is the continuing story of Melanie. It will help you better understand the effect of a diagnosis of ALS on a person's life and why raising funds for research and care is critical. The ALS Ice Bucket Challenge helped, but there is still more to be done.

MELANIE'S STORY CONTINUES: FROM SYMPTOMS TO DIAGNOSIS

When we last heard from Melanie, she had become aware of a tingling sensation in her hand. Melanie said, "It was in November of 2016, as I was preparing for my son Christopher's wedding, that I realized I didn't have strength in my hand. I wanted to wear something in my hair, like a jeweled bobby pin, for the wedding, but I couldn't put it on. My right hand was not strong enough to get the bobby pin in my hair." In the excitement of the wedding, this incident was pushed away. But Melanie knew she needed to determine what was causing the weakness.

"It was at that point that I mentioned it to my doctor at an appointment in December of 2016. The doctor thought, 'Well, you might be a little arthritic; maybe your hands are affected by that.' It was kind of really brushed off; it wasn't anything serious. But to me, it was concerning. As 2017 approached, I called the nurse and said, 'My hand is weak, I'm not in pain, it's just weak. I'd really like to have it checked out.' So, my doctor decided to send me to a neurologist in a local practice."

At this point, Melanie went for several tests, including IgG (CSF Immunoglobulin G (IgG) index). Melanie said, "My regular doctor said it could be Multiple Sclerosis (MS), maybe you have a type of MS. The new doctor I had did the test; I was there alone. I wasn't expecting anything earth-shattering. The other thing they had tested me for was Lyme disease, which was negative. So, I wasn't really concerned, or I wouldn't have been alone. I mentioned what my regular doctor had said. And this doctor said, 'No, you don't have MS. I believe you have ALS,' and she kind of just blurted it out. And I was like, 'Oh, well, that's bad.'

"I left that office, and I went down to the car and called my husband. And I, of course, told him what she said. I started to cry and say, 'That's crazy. I can't believe she just told me that.' As I drove back to work that day, I had so many things racing through my head; I was in shock, of course, not wanting to believe that could be the diagnosis I was going to be facing. I remember I pulled over to call my doctor's office to dial the number. I drove away after I got her on speakerphone, but I just explained to her what was told to me and I believe she was in shock, also.

"You know, I don't remember her ever mentioning ALS to me. She did mention MS. I think that's what she thought I was going to be dealing with. I explained to her at that time that I had no intention of going back to that doctor, because I was very unhappy with the way she handled the situation, knowing I was alone and giving me that kind of information. I don't know how she should have handled it, but I know that wasn't the way. She agreed and said we would figure it out from there. I hung up with her and then I arrived back at work. Of course, I have a busy job, but I did sit down at my computer right away, in my office, and I researched, and I found that there was a multidisciplinary clinic at Lahey Hospital and Clinic in Burlington, MA. I was very familiar with Lahey Burlington, so I knew right away, that's where I needed to start.

"For the rest of the day, I worked. I had a busy job, plenty to do, and I went home that night. The hardest part was thinking about not just myself but having to tell people about the diagnosis.

"In June, I was diagnosed by my neurologist at Lahey Clinic, Dr. Doreen Ho. She suggested that I have a second opinion, which really would have been a third opinion at this point, and I agreed. I ended up getting an appointment, in the neurology department at Massachusetts General Hospital, which is very difficult to do. I saw Dr. James Berry, and he confirmed the diagnosis. He did say I could go to Mass General to a multidisciplinary clinic. However, he knew Dr. Doreen

Ho, and he said he felt that I would be in great hands with her. Really just for convenience sake, and that I really liked Lahey Burlington. I said, 'I'll just stick there.' It's convenient, but if I thought I was going to get better quality care at Mass General, I probably would have gone there. The care I've received has been nothing but excellent. I don't regret that decision. I know I always have Mass General available to me if I need. So, that was the craziness of my diagnosis.

SHARING THE NEWS

"By now, it was June of 2017. At this point, my right hand was weaker than it had been, but that was really the only symptom that I was showing at the time. Our next task was to get the news to everyone. We have a great support system: wonderful friends, dear friends, and we have a loving family on both sides, and two children.

"Having to tell everyone was very difficult because the news of ALS is difficult enough. It was challenging to explain because at the time, I really didn't have any signs except for my right hand. My right hand was starting to fold in on itself. You could see it if I showed it to you and pointed it out. People would say, 'Well, how do they know you have ALS?' I explained the tests, and then I'd show my hand. They'd say, 'Oh, yeah, I see it, I guess.'

"People ask, 'Well, what do they do for it?' People want to know, 'What's the treatment?' There really isn't a treatment, not a treatment or a cure. There are a couple of medicines that can increase your lifespan by a few months, but everything has side effects.

"Unfortunately, the life expectancy for a diagnose of ALS is two to five years. This doesn't account for how long it has been brewing. Who knows? I had the tingling in my hands for all those years. Could that possibly have been the start of it? I don't know. I don't think I've ever gotten an answer if it was, but the deterioration of my right hand was clear and was pretty fast. Most of my other symptoms came on at a slower pace.

"It's a frustrating diagnosis because there's not much you can do. You try to live your best life and stay as positive as possible."

We'll learn more about what this diagnosis means for changes to Melanie's life in the coming chapters.

CHAPTER 6

GOING VIRAL: THE ALS ICE BUCKET CHALLENGE IS BORN

Remember when we heard from Melanie about her experience with the ALS Ice Bucket Challenge? Knowing a bit about the backstory of the ALS Ice Bucket Challenge in the United States is helpful. While many people became aware of it in July and August 2014, other individuals and groups had been doing something similar to raise money for charities they supported. In the early days, the challenge was not connected to any specific organization, including ALSA. This wasn't something that started out viral, and it became linked to ALS much later.

The *Wall Street Journal* found that professional golfers had been using what they called the cold water challenge to raise funds to support specific charities in which they had a personal interest. In May 2014, firefighters from the Washington Township, New Jersey Fire Department posted a

YouTube video of themselves getting sprayed with firehoses, which resulted in their being called out because they used equipment without permission.[43] People began doing the cold water challenge as a way to raise money for causes and charities, but not specifically ALS. Pat Quinn had used the Ice Bucket Challenge with his Quinn for the Win advocacy and fundraising efforts for ALS in 2013.[44] It was Pete Frates and Pat Quinn who connected the challenge with ALS.

Pete Frates was diagnosed with ALS on March 13, 2012, when he was twenty-seven years old.[45] Pete was an incredible athlete and had done very well in high school in a wide variety of sports, including baseball, hockey, and football. "Growing up in Beverly, Massachusetts, sports were at the forefront of everything I did and strived toward. While football and hockey were likewise things that came easily to me, baseball was my one true love."[46] Though recruited by several colleges, his dream had been to go to Boston College, his parents' alma mater, and play baseball.

Studying communications and history enabled him to pursue what he loved: sports. Pete was known for making good friends and having fun, but he worked hard and pushed himself with workouts and training. Ultimately, he earned the honor of being the captain of the baseball team in his

---

43 Sumathi Reddy, "How the Ice-Bucket Challenge Got Its Start," *Wall Street Journal,* August 14, 2014.

44 "Quinn for the Win," ALS Therapy Development Institute, accessed September 27, 2020.

45 Pete Frates, "My Journey from Baseball Star to ALS Patient, 75 Years After Lou Gehrig," *Bleacherreport*.com, July 2, 2014.

46 Ibid.

senior year. During his time at Boston College, he built a large network of sports-minded friends who admired his natural leadership abilities and reputation for perseverance and optimism. These friends would become a crucial part of sharing the news of the ALS Ice Bucket Challenge.[47]

Pete was in college when Facebook first appeared, and he became intrigued. Though Facebook was originally only for students at Harvard and then a few other Ivy League colleges, Boston College was soon added to the network. Pete quickly moved on to other types of social media, including Twitter and Instagram, leaving Facebook behind. At the time, he did not realize the role Facebook would play for him in the future. This early adoption of social media and its networking capabilities, along with Pete's interest in how it was used, would come to play a large role in the speed and growth of the ALS Ice Bucket Challenge.[48]

From early in his diagnosis, which occurred after college, Pete knew that he wanted to help people understand ALS and raise funds for ALS research. Though many people knew that Lou Gehrig was a great major league baseball player and had ALS, Pete had a special understanding of what Gehrig had faced. He was upset that nothing had changed or improved since Gehrig was diagnosed in 1939. Was it the low numbers of people diagnosed? ALS.org notes, "Based on US population studies, a little over 5,000 people in the US are diagnosed with ALS each year. (That's 15 new cases a day.)

47 Casey Sherman and Dave Wedge, *The Ice Bucket Challenge: Pete Frates and the Fight against ALS*, (Lebanon, NH: University Press of New England, 2017), 35.

48 Sherman and Wedge, *The Ice Bucket Challenge*, 39.

Every 90 minutes, someone is diagnosed with the disease and someone passes away from it. It is estimated that at least 16,000 have the disease at any given time."[49]

According to ALS.org, "Only four drugs are currently FDA-approved to treat ALS: Riluzole, Nuedexta, Radicava, and Tiglutik. Nuedexta is approved to treat pseudobulbar affect, difficulty with emotional control, including inappropriate laughing and crying, which impacts some people with ALS. The estimated cost to develop a drug to slow or stop the progression of ALS from an idea to an approved drug is between $2 billion and $3 billion."[50] For comparison, the number of people diagnosed with cancer each year is 1.7 million. In *Cancer Today*, Dr.George Demetri wrote, "In September 2018, Congress passed a fiscal year 2019 spending bill that included $39.1 billion for the NIH and $6.14 billion for the NCI."[51]

Pete asked his doctor, Dr. Merit Cudkowicz, chief of neurology at Massachusetts General Hospital, about what it would cost to do the research to find a cure for ALS. A billion dollars was the answer.[52] Pete took the answer as a challenge to raise awareness and the funding to find a cure. Knowing a cure was unlikely to be found in time for him didn't slow his drive to make it better for others.

---

49 "What is ALS?" als.org, Accessed April 6, 2020.

50 Ibid.

51 George Demetri, "Public Funding is the Lifeblood of Cancer Research. *CancerTodayMag*, Accessed April 3, 2020.

52 Sherman and Wedge, *The Ice Bucket Challenge*, 75.

As Pete's condition progressed, he started the Pete Frates #3 Fund to further his mission to raise awareness of and funding for ALS research and to help defray some of the costs of his care. Family members joined in to build a website and handle the financials of the organization, and friends joined the call. The team became known as Team Frate Train, and Pete's brother, Andrew, took to social media to get the message out.[53]

By 2013, Facebook had changed considerably since Pete's experience with it in college, with more people of all age groups using it. Emil Protalinski of The NextWeb stated, "While sharing its financial results for its third quarter, Facebook today announced a number of new milestones. The social network has now passed 1.19 billion monthly active users. Of those, daily active users passed 728 million on average during September 2013, and the number of monthly active mobile users hit 874 million."[54] In addition, Leo Widrich of *Buffer* found that while the typical user was female and between the ages of eighteen and twenty-nine, 73 percent of thirty- to forty-nine-year-olds, 57 percent of fifty- to sixty-four-year-olds, and 35 percent of people aged sixty-five and older were using Facebook.[55] Team Frate Train began to see Facebook as a tremendous networking and marketing tool that would raise awareness of ALS and inform the public of fundraising events through a variety of channels.

---

53 Sherman and Wedge, *The Ice Bucket Challenge*, 102.

54 Emil Protalinski, "Facebook passes 1.19 billion monthly active users, 874 million mobile users, and 728 million daily users," *The Next Web*, Oct 30, 2013.

55 Leo Widrich, "Social Media in 2013: User Demographics For Twitter, Facebook, Pinterest and Instagram," *Buffer* (blog), May 2, 2013.

Twitter was also a social media choice for Team Frate Train, and the ability to use hashtags escalated the reach of these events. The power of these tools cannot be underestimated, as they opened up new ways to connect with people and raise awareness of ALS.

The first use of a hashtag (#) is credited to Chris Messina, who invented the hashtag in 2007, "...changing the social media landscape forever by providing a means to galvanize popular social movements."[56] Looking back at the influence of the hashtag in 2018, Ben Panko stated, "The hashtag was intended to be a type of metadata tag that allowed users to apply dynamic, user-generated tagging, which made it possible for others to easily find messages with a specific theme or content. It allowed easy, informal markup of folksonomy without the need for any formal taxonomy or markup language"[57] Using a hashtag allowed people to easily search and identify with particular groups of interest to them.

Team Frate Train began using the tags #StrikeOutALS and #TeamFrateTrain to spread the news about ALS and build awareness. According to Sherman and Wedge, "'The man upstairs has given me a plan,' Pete told them. 'I knew my gifts were not being used when I was an insurance salesman. Once I was diagnosed, it clicked. This is it. This is my calling. This is what I've been put here to do. The reason why there are no effective treatments for ALS, as there now are for HIV and cancer, is that we ALS patients are not around long enough

---

56 Chris Messina, On a Mission to Make Myself Useful, nd.

57 Ben Panko, "A Decade Ago, the Hashtag Reshaped the Internet," *Smithsonian*. August 23, 2017.

to make a stink to let people know that, hey, we're here and we need a treatment and a cure. We are in a gunfight without a gun and not even a knife. We are fighting with a plastic spork.'"[58]

Pete continued to network with other ALS patients, and he was able to help them with their battle against ALS by providing support and encouragement. Still, he knew he needed to raise significant money and awareness if there were ever to be a cure for ALS.

Anthony Senerchia was diagnosed with ALS in 2003 and had lived with it for eleven years when the normal life expectancy was two to five years. His wife Jeanette's cousin, Chris Kennedy, was a pro golfer and is credited with bringing ALSA to the challenge of pouring a bucket of ice water over his head. He called out Jeanette and two friends and challenged them to do it, saying if they didn't do it, they would have to pay $100 to ALSA.[59]

A video was posted to Facebook where Jeanette saw it. With some coaxing from Kennedy, Jeanette took him up on the challenge, and tagged a friend of Pat Quinn, another ALS patient. Pat took the challenge and tagged Pete Frates, his mentor, friend, and fellow ALS patient.[60] This was a significant moment, as Pete Frates understood this could be what he had hoped for: the potential to reach a lot of people through

58 Sherman and Wedge, *The Ice Bucket Challenge*, 103.

59 Alexandra Sifferlin, "Here's How the ALS Ice Bucket Challenge Actually Started," *Time*, August 18, 2014.

60 Ibid.

social media. The Ice Bucket Challenge, up until this point, had not been connected to ALS specifically but was being used as a way to raise money for a variety of causes. Pete saw an opportunity and asked his mom to get on social media and start liking, sharing, and commenting on all the videos of people taking the challenge. He convinced his dad and brother to do the challenge and call out three people and challenge them, too. Very quickly, traffic to Pete's website increased.

Sherman and Wedge said, "For the first twenty-four hours, Nancy, Julie, and John barely left their seats at the kitchen table. The videos started coming in once every half hour. Soon they were coming in every half second. They liked, tagged, commented, and shared hundreds of videos that came pouring in. Pete served as the field general, barking orders through his computer and offering words of encouragement to his troops. He then emailed every professional athlete, politician, and influencer he knew and urged them all to join his team."[61]

Remember, at this time, there was no Donate button on Facebook. Participants were encouraged to go to Pete's website to donate. As part of their strategy, they added other ALS organizations to their home page, including the ALS Foundation, Compassionate Care ALS, the Angel Fund, and the ALS Therapy Development Institute.[62] This was intended to help people educate themselves about ALS to learn more about the disease and how they could help. An outpouring

---

61 Sherman and Wedge, *The Ice Bucket Challenge*, 112.

62 Sherman and Wedge, *The Ice Bucket Challenge*, 114.

of support from so many people came through letters, cards, and videos. It also gave those who had known someone with ALS a chance to share their experiences and help with the fight for a cure for ALS.

When you know someone who has been diagnosed with ALS and start to learn about the disease, you can easily feel disheartened by the outcome. Through social media, Team Frate Train allowed people to connect and receive support. They could share their messages and thoughts as they participated in the challenge. And they did! Over and over again, through social media, furthering the understanding and knowledge of ALS.

While a few people prior to the Ice Bucket Challenge knew what ALS stood for, many still related it to Lou Gehrig and did not fully comprehend the meaning of the diagnosis. After all, it had been seventy-five years since Gehrig had died, and although baseball and sports aficionados may have been familiar with the term ALS, few other people knew of the disease unless they knew of or knew someone who had been diagnosed. No effective treatments or cure had happened in all that time! ALS is not like cancer, which practically every one of us knows someone impacted. The Ice Bucket Challenge raised awareness of a disease in a manner that set it apart from other awareness and advocacy campaigns in large part due to its effective call to action that resonated with so many people.

Realizing what a role the *challenge* aspect played in this is important. By asking each person taking the challenge to call out three friends to also take it, the message spread quickly across social media. As it extended throughout the world, celebrities like Justin Timberlake took the challenge and then challenged more celebrities. Jimmy Fallon, Oprah Winfrey, Taylor Swift, Steven Spielberg, and others challenged their friends to participate. This contributed to the attention the ALS Ice Bucket Challenge was receiving.

WHAT IT WAS LIKE FROM AN ORGANIZATIONAL PERSPECTIVE

Pete Frates and Team Frate Train were just one part of the equation. On the other side, what was happening in the national offices of ALSA in Washington, DC? The ALS Ice Bucket Challenge's popularity seemingly came out of nowhere. I spoke with Carrie Munk, who described her experience as senior vice president of communications and marketing of ALSA. "I was in an off-site fundraising meeting with my colleagues, and it was one of those half-day planning sessions that you plan three months in advance. Lynn Aaronson, who is currently the executive director of the DC-Maryland-Virginia chapter of the ALS Association, but at the time was with the Massachusetts Chapter, gave me a call and said, 'Carrie, something big is going on here!'"

According to Munk, Aaronson had just done her own Ice Bucket Challenge on camera with a local Boston television station and encouraged her to keep an eye on the national situation because the challenge was really taking off in Boston and beginning to reach other parts of the country. Munk continued, "After I got the call from Lynn, I asked my fundraising colleagues, 'Has anyone taken a look at our donations the last couple of days?'"

Munk noted, "This was in the middle of August, and sure enough, we looked at the income statements, and I believe we were about $50,000 ahead of where we were in a previous year. We thought that was really odd. In the nonprofit world, in many, many cases, August is the doldrums of fundraising; that's why you have your off-site planning meetings because everyone's on vacation and getting ready to go back to school. Within the next two to three to four days, my colleagues were taking a look at the books and saying, 'Okay, people are donating at a rate we've never seen before in August.' At one point in time, there were several consecutive days during a thirty-day period where we brought in over $10 million a day, unheard of sums of money, it was just completely unheard of."

Just managing the volume of media interest was challenging. Munk contacted a colleague at Porter Novelli who reached out to Brian Frederick, who today is head of creative at ALSA Washington, DC. At the time of the ALS Ice Bucket Challenge, Frederick was working for Porter Novelli as vice president of public affairs. Frederick said, "There was a lot of interest, media requests, and donations. I volunteered to come over and talk with them [ALS Association] and help them. Immediately I started just helping to triage media requests, handle basic press releases and talking points, social media, and correspondence to try and keep it going. One of the things I insisted upon was every time we referred to the challenge in interviews, press releases, and social media, we called it the ALS Ice Bucket Challenge. I think that our strategy was never to get out ahead of it, but to be behind the scenes doing everything we could. Some of that remained sort of an organic community driven campaign. But, you know, we tactically did some things to help fan those flames and it became a worldwide phenomenon; it was an amazing summer, for sure."

Munk said, "I feel so fortunate to have been part of it. I had spent many years at the American Red Cross, and it was completely different, the circumstances of the unprecedented giving. One of the things I stressed at the time, that I learned when I was at the Red Cross, was that when something like this is happening, business as usual doesn't exist. You have to adapt; you have to innovate. For us, it was a tricky situation because we were so fortunate that people were directing their giving to the ALS Association. We had to be flexible. For example, I spent a lot of time correcting misinformation because people thought we started it. No, we didn't start this. This is an organic movement; it's these three guys who were living with this disease and they're so incredible. Our public relations strategy at the time was really to embrace the campaign and give people the tools that they needed to keep it going. We never took our eyes away from ultimately what the mission of our organization is at the ALS Association. I think that was particularly helpful at the time."

One of the striking things that set the ALS Ice Bucket Challenge apart was how quickly the ALSA engaged with participants and donors. Munk said, "We wanted to express gratitude, which was part of our strategy because people were taking time out of their day to do this kind of silly thing, which was so serious in the long run as far as support for people with the disease. It's exciting to see the progress made in research since then."

The ALS Ice Bucket Challenge garnered energy because from the beginning challenge, it was a call to action that resonated personally with so many people. The ALSA recognized very early on that *using a strategy to not just pursue dollars, but to pursue educating and informing participants was a way to increase engagement when the challenge ended.* They knew they had to retain interest so that it did not become a one-off type of event, but rather laid a foundation for future awareness and support.

All of this leads into the next section that looks at how social media goes viral, an elusive concept without any written rules on how to make it happen. Are there certain factors that collide and provide the opportunity to become viral? Let's take a look.

WHAT DOES IT MEAN TO GO VIRAL?

We've all heard the term "go viral," but have you ever asked yourself, "How does this happen?" "Is it intentional?" "How does it become a phenomenon?" Robert Wynne from *Forbes* magazine interviewed Jonah Berger, a professor at the Wharton School of the University of Pennsylvania and the author of *Invisible Influence: The Hidden Forces That Shape Behavior*, who explained, "Unfortunately there is no hard and fast definition."

"Further, people often use viral to mean highly shared, but what it really often means is popular. A video can get a million views because a brand paid to have it placed on various sites. That's why I talk about how contagious something is, or how likely it is to be shared given exposure."[63]

How many people have to view a post before it is viral? Is it one hundred thousand views? A million views? Does it count if those views are bought or paid for, because that is one way to make sure a post is seen. Depending on the post, either one of those may be a measure of validity. Robert Wynne stated, "As I like to define success by actual performance, I suggest being listed/tagged on a major social networks 'trending' section. Facebook has one on their home page, and Twitter as well. YouTube, Tumblr, Instagram, and Snapchat, that would signal to me that something is trending at a level of importance."[64]

According to Dr. Spencer Ross, assistant professor of marketing at the University of Massachusetts Lowell, "People had an intuitive notion of viral marketing, about the need to make things go viral or and what makes things go viral. Viral one-offs existed, even prior to social media. You had buzz and word of mouth, both of which encompassed viral marketing, but in 2014, you started to see where people became more aware of its use on social media. When the Ice Bucket Challenge happened, people started to pay a bit more attention to the actual features of viral content and the social psychology behind why it occurs online and what is happening with social transmission. This even gets into a deeper understanding of meme culture. It's not that memes

---

63 Robert Wynne, "There Are No Guarantees—Or Exact Statistics—For Going Viral," *Forbes*, March 9, 2018.

64 Ibid.

didn't previously exist, but I think it's probably around 2014 that both researchers and practitioners started to look at why memes piqued a lot of marketers' interest in terms of how can we leverage what other people know."

Think of your own experiences of viewing or sharing posts that have gone viral. What was it about the post that made you want to share? Did the post evoke something you found humorous and thought others would find funny, too? Did it pull at your heartstrings? How did you feel when you shared the post, but others didn't always respond to it the same way you did? Did fear play a role in your need to share? Again, how did you react when you saw people's responses? As individuals, we all have different ways of reacting to what we see. Some of these have nothing at all to do with the actual post, but rather with how we are feeling that day and what might be going on at the moment we viewed the post. Angry at your partner? Having a good day? Feeling appreciated? Each of these types of emotions will result in a different experience of what we see and how we feel.

Jonah Berger, author of *Contagious: Why Things Catch On*, starts off a podcast at Wharton with this: "The easiest place to start would be cats. [If you ask], 'Why do things go viral?' people usually give one of two answers. They say, 'Oh, it's random. It's luck. It's just chance.' Or they say, 'It's cats.' If you look on the web, there are viral cat pictures, so it must be cats that drive things to go viral. There are definitely some cat things that become popular, but that really doesn't tell us anything about why most things go viral. It doesn't tell us why some cat videos are shared, and others aren't, and it doesn't tell us why things that have nothing to do with cats go viral. It's like noticing that Bill Gates, Bill Cosby, and Bill Clinton are all names that start with 'Bill' and deciding to name your child Bill because that will make them famous. It's messing up correlation and causation."[65]

Berger's research on why we share things is helpful in understanding how the ALS Ice Bucket Challenge garnered so many participants worldwide through sharing posts. He developed six steps that he uses to show what drives people to engage with and share posts, and he created them with the acronym STEPPS.

- "**Social currency:** It's all about people talking about things to make themselves look good, rather than bad.
- **Triggers**, which is all about the idea of 'top of mind, tip of tongue.' We talk about things that are on the top of our heads.
- **Ease for Emotion:** When we care, we share. The more we care about a piece of information or the more we're feeling physiologically aroused, the more likely we pass something on.
- **Public:** When we can see other people doing something, we're more likely to imitate it.
- **Practical value:** Basically, it's the idea of news you can use. We share information to help others, to make them better off.
- **Stories,** or how we share things that are often wrapped up in stories or narratives."[66]

---

65 Jonah Berger, "'Contagious': Jonah Berger on Why Things Catch On," March 13, 2013, In Knowledge@Wharton, Podcast Transcript. P2.

66 Ibid.

Using this framework, let's evaluate Berger's STEPPS in terms of the ALS Ice Bucket Challenge:

- **Social currency:** Supporting a nonprofit is a plus in social currency—you're doing something to help someone else. By participating you are saying you care about others, and you want to show people how they can care, too.
- **Triggers:** The more people who see the video, the more people who will be reminded of what ALS is and why you need to raise money for research.
- **Ease for Emotion:** The experience of dumping cold water over your head will likely stay with you for a long time. It will make it easier for us to have empathy for those with ALS and help us become more comfortable discussing why it is important to cure ALS.
- **Public:** Being publicly challenged to participate makes us more likely to take the challenge. In addition, because people videotaped themselves doing it, there is a desire to join with others in the challenge because it would be seen in a positive manner.
- **Practical value:** If we can raise awareness of ALS, along with the need to raise money to find effective treatments and a cure, we can improve and extend the lives of others.
- **Stories:** Every video told a story—*your story*—about why you wanted to do the challenge. If you knew someone with ALS, you could recognize them publicly, so that others felt connected to a deeper meaning behind the challenge.

As we can see, the ALS Ice Bucket Challenge had all the elements of STEPPS Berger outlined, which helped drive the participation of individuals to share their experience on social media. Every time we saw someone complete the challenge, it resonated with us and activated feelings of wanting to contribute and be a part of something big.

Think about how social media posts can spread and take on a life of their own, going beyond what the initial intention of the post may have been. As seen above, Berger provides an excellent framework to understand how posts can spread through engagement. However, in the very beginning, there may seem to be no predictable direction. Before the ALS Ice Bucket Challenge, several well-known athletes were using the cold water challenge to raise money for charities they supported. The Polar Plunge Boston is a similar type of event, in which people jump into the cold Atlantic Ocean on New Year's Day to raise money for the Special Olympics.

Lorna Boucher, chief marketing officer for Instinet, noted, "Social media works best when there's almost an organic community that forms. There's a strange thing that happens in the social ecosphere. It's like murmuration; you know how birds, swallows flying in flocks, just randomly shift one way and then shift another way. You can see everybody following everybody else, but what is the trigger that made them all go in that direction? The truth is most people don't have any idea what causes a big murmuration. If you can recognize when a murmuration is happening, rightly recognize when something dramatic and organic is happening, you can learn from and lean into that opportunity."

This idea of murmuration, of a groundswell of interest and actions that take place, is interesting. Boucher's point of being able to recognize when this is starting can provide notification that there may be an opportunity to exploit. Pete Frates saw this when videos of people taking the challenge and sharing them began to show up on his computer. It was the signal of murmuration, a movement that gains followers. Frates stated, "'I've been preaching, calling for mobilization and the opportunity to raise money to fight ALS on a mass scale. I've been developing and building a large and powerful network of supporters and influencers for this very reason.'"[67]

The ALS Ice Bucket Challenge had barely begun, but Pete knew this moment was the break he had been looking for Team Frate Train. Quinn has expressed similar comments about his Quinn for the Win supporters. This was a critical moment for Team Frate Train, and much of the results of the ALS Ice Bucket Challenge are due to Frates' and Quinn's early identification of this enigma.

---

67 Sherman and Wedge, *The Ice Bucket Challenge: Pete Frates and the Fight against ALS*, 111.

CHAPTER 7

I NEED A MARKETING PLAN?

Imagine driving from Boston to California with no maps and no GPS, just heading west and hoping it works out alright. Would you get there faster, use less gas, and take more direct routes if you used a map or GPS? Most likely, yes. ***Similarly, do you need a marketing plan? Yes, you do!*** You want to reach your goal efficiently with the lowest investment in time and energy. A marketing plan will keep you on track and let your organization know what you want to accomplish. You need a target to hit, which can be to gain new donors, volunteers, or clients. Perhaps you want more constituents, additional fundraising, or awareness campaigns. The list goes on and on, but you need a marketing plan if you want to be successful.

Some of the more traditional types of marketing materials small nonprofits use include newsletters, brochures, flyers, letters, and mailings. You want to integrate social media across all of your printed material that the public will see.

Draw a diagram or chart to show how these all relate to each other and keep it in a prominent place where all your employees can see it. Below is an example. You can customize this template to your nonprofit. There's a full-color version available at https://wakeupcall.finchfamily.org/YouAreA-Marketer.pdf. After all, your employees and volunteers are your best marketing tool!

YOU ARE A MARKETER!

OUR ORGANIZATION WORKS IN UNISON TO ACHIEVE OUR MISSION

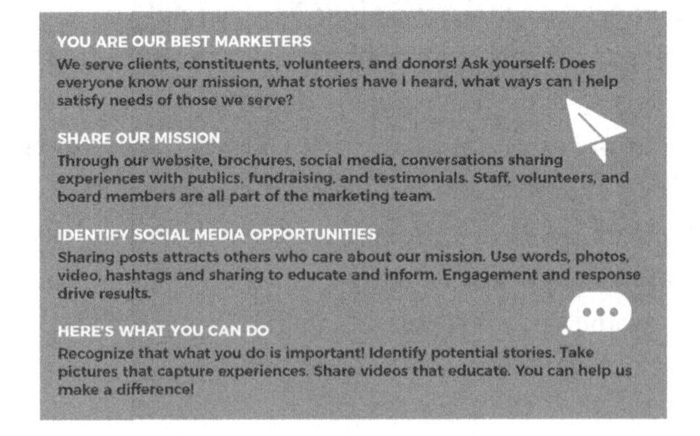

Figure 1: *You Are A Marketer! This poster can be placed in a common area that your staff and volunteers frequent. It is intended to help them understand and recognize their role in marketing your organization and how they can help.*

Now, I'm not here to tell you how to write a marketing plan. There are any number of good books and online sites that can help you with that. However, I am going to tell you about a piece of the marketing plan I don't believe is emphasized enough. **You need an Action Plan!** That's right, a real live document that everyone who is part of your team can access and provide input, to ensure that you accomplish everything you want to do. It should contain periodic metrics for each activity to know when resources need to be reallocated. This is key to any marketing or other type of plan, including strategic planning. A social media action plan might include in table format the action type, any details need, frequency of posting, metrics, evaluation, and goals. This could be a weekly or monthly planner, and there are online templates available to help you.

In my nonprofit marketing class, I often find the action plan is the missing piece when students develop a marketing plan. They do the research needed to develop a marketing plan, but for some reason, the actual implementation of a written plan is often left unmentioned or glossed over lightly. *Don't make this mistake!* The assumption that having written a marketing plan is all you need to do is very common, both by students and nonprofit organizations. I will emphasize again here that smaller nonprofits are more likely to struggle with this than larger nonprofits with marketing departments or personnel in place.

I find keeping action plans in a table or Excel is most useful, though feel free to choose your own method. It should be accessible at any time. Here's a suggestion of how to get started:

- **Step 1:** Define your end goal
- **Step 2:** List the steps to be followed
- **Step 3:** Prioritize tasks and add deadlines
- **Step 4:** Set milestones
- **Step 5:** Identify the resources needed
- **Step 6:** Visualize your action plan
- **Step 7:** Monitor, evaluate, and update

Also, make sure that you have categories that include:

- What needs to be done—be specific
- Who is going to do it—assign it to an individual or a group
- Metrics to measure progress
- When it will be completed—pick an estimated date, but be flexible enough to change the date, if needed
- Who is going to ensure that everyone stays on track—the person who is in charge of making sure the plan is progressing

Action plans help everyone in the nonprofit see and know what has been done, what is being done, and when it is done. This is important because we all know how easy it is to get overwhelmed with day-to-day tasks, and then suddenly a few weeks have flown by and we've forgotten all about what we intended to complete. Having a visual reminder, along with a weekly or biweekly check-in, can help everyone, including staff, administrators, board members, and volunteers, commit to helping the nonprofit reach its marketing goals.

SOCIAL MEDIA AS A PART OF THE MARKETING PLAN

Once you have an overview of the marketing plan for the nonprofit, you should make social media an integral part of the plan. Social media is in a tremendous growth period! Today, with so many people of all ages utilizing social media, determining a social media plan that aligns with the marketing plan of the organization is important to helping it reach its marketing goals.

I spoke with LZ Nunn, executive director of Project LEARN in Lowell, Massachusetts, and asked her to describe how she worked with her marketing staff person. She said, "We set goals on the number of touches, the number of news items, the number of social media followers, and the number of fundraising asks. We set those goals and created a six-month plan. We had routine meetings about marketing once a week, in terms of what we were doing next and what our plans were. A lot of it was about building energy, based on programs we support. Early on, we focused less on Project LEARN's story and more on student impact stories for the STEM-based programs we were raising money to fund. Donors want to hear inspiring stories about young people, and once we focused on those, we had more success raising funds through our marketing efforts." By doing this, Project LEARN was able to focus their social media marketing on the areas that generated the greatest interest.

Just as we need a template to communicate the marketing plan, we also need one for social media. Below is a way to help organizations think about what they want to gain from their social media posts, how they can be sure that they are including all aspects of their goals, and which social media channels are best for each goal. You can customize this template to your nonprofit. There's a full-color version available at *https://wakeupcall.finchfamily.org/PowerOfSocialMedia.pdf.*

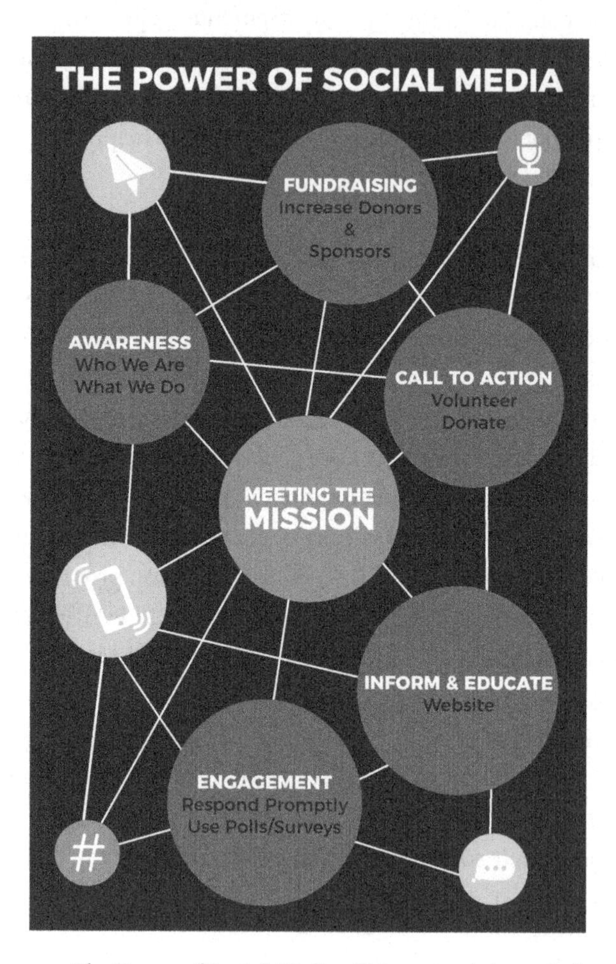

Figure 2: *The Power of Social Media: This poster is intended to convey to staff and volunteers the importance of the activities of social media to the organization's mission. It is an interconnected relationship that grounds all activities and opportunities to the mission.*

DO WE NEED A SOCIAL MEDIA COORDINATOR?

A common social media marketing problem in smaller nonprofit organizations is the tendency to make posts for the sake of making a post, not for alignment with the goals of the organization. Many posts are opportunistic rather than strategic. Remember, **"More Posts' Is Not a Strategy!" #MPINS** This mistake is not intentional, but it is often the result of *not* having someone specifically in charge of social media. Granted, we know nonprofits are often strapped for time and staff resources, but relying on everyone and anyone in the organization to post to social media can limit its effectiveness in reaching your goals. You need to be sure your organization's brand is communicated in a consistent manner. I advocate choosing one person to make sure all posts are helping meet the goals. This doesn't mean others can't post; it just means that before staff post, they check in with the social media coordinator to ensure the post conveys the goals of the organization.

Why is this so important? I've given some good reasons above, but I want you to think about posts you've seen that have spelling or grammatical errors. What was your takeaway from seeing those? Does it say something about the organization—a lack of attention to detail? To many people, it does. For example, if I'm a donor, I might wonder about how they'll use my donation, or if they are financially responsible with the nonprofit's funds. If you misspell a volunteer's name in the post, what message are you sending to that volunteer? Errors make people second-guess a decision they might have been comfortable with before.

A social media coordinator can provide consistency in communication of the organization because they have a big-picture idea of how to connect marketing to the goals of the nonprofit. This is why it is important to have the right person for the job. You do not necessarily need someone with a background in marketing and social media, but the person must be able to learn about marketing and understand how social media can help the organization achieve its goals and how it aligns with the marketing plan.

I have witnessed nonprofits that rely on an intern or college student to manage their social media accounts, assuming that because they are young and use social media, they will know what to do. This is not always true! Yes, the intern may use social media for their own use, but *managing your personal social media is quite different than managing it for a business.* Saying a young person should know how to market a nonprofit on social media because they know how to use social media is like saying they should be able to write a letter to a donor because they know how to use a pen. Many times, they have had little or no experience with marketing any type of business, for-profit or nonprofit! Don't expect them to know or understand this if they have never done it before. Learning about an organization and what it does, beyond the programs and services offered, takes time.

In some cases, an intern may be unaware of the rules about using images of children or people with disabilities, who may be a component of the people the nonprofit serves. These rules need to be included in an onboarding program for new employees. In an article about ethics in nonprofit photography, photographer Margot Duane stated, "Even though images created for nonprofit campaigns aren't being created or published for typically commercial applications, it's strongly recommended that precautions are taken around permissions. If creating images, one should obtain model releases whenever possible, especially if there is a chance that the person pictured may experience negative consequences as a result of having their photo used. If the subject isn't able to read the release or sign his/her name, an interpreter should be made available to explain the intended use of the photography. If stock photos are being used, one should confirm that the proper releases are in place: make no assumptions."[68] In addition, make sure you have written permission from the parents or guardian of minors whose photographs are being used.

Do not make the mistake of naming someone social media coordinator without being certain they understand marketing and branding the organization. Branding is critical in conveying the image of the organization to its public. It needs to be consistent and send a professional message about what your organization does. One way to do this is to communicate to everyone in the organization the need for cohesion in all messaging. This means using colors, fonts, and images that reflect positively on the organization. You want to always include a link to the nonprofit's website so viewers can learn more about the organization. Utilize a Donate button, prominently displayed, so no one needs to search for it. Nothing is more frustrating to someone who wants to donate money

---

68 Margot Duane, "Nonprofit Photography: Ethics and Approaches," *The Community Network*, accessed June 16, 2020.

than finding they have to spend time looking for a way to donate. You want to make it as easy as possible!

BUILDING A CONTENT CALENDAR

A busy nonprofit (I've never seen one that is not busy!), needs a way to manage social media that relies on prior planning. Enter the content calendar: a way to schedule and manage your social media posts in a timely manner. The nonprofits that I believe successfully provide social media content use a content calendar. Luckily, using a content calendar is not difficult. There are many great products and templates that will allow you to promote the organization on a regular schedule. Microsoft Excel, Google Drive, Loomly, Trello, Hootsuite, HubSpot, and Sprout Social make available free or low-cost content calendars.

This type of planning allows you to organize and customize content and distribution to best meet your nonprofit's goals. Using a content calendar enables you to set up automatic posts on a monthly basis, or more frequently if needed. It allows the social media coordinator to focus on how cohesive the messaging can be because it is done well in advance, rather than on a day-to-day or week-to-week schedule. Consistency matters! A content calendar helps you do this.[69]

You can also take advantage of the wide variety of themes, holidays, and events, many you might never have been aware of before! Did you know there is a National Siblings Day,

---

69 Paige Cooper & Shannon Tien, "How to Create a Social Media Content Calendar: Tips and Templates," Hootsuite Social Media Management (Blog), January 23, 2020.

Star Wars Day, World Nutella Day, International Dance Day, and World Television Day?[70] By tying your posts into one of these themes, you are also able to increase exposure through hashtags. Just remember, you need to relate these themes to your nonprofit and its mission. Not everything will be a good fit, but there are plenty of ways to add interest to your posts and gain more attention.

It all comes down to the "Why."

---

70 Sameer Panjwani, "12 Months Of Content Event Triggers For Your Editorial Calendar," Search Engine People (Blog), December 9, 2014.

PART TWO

PUTTING IT INTO PRACTICE

CHAPTER 8

HOW TO TELL YOUR WHY

How do you become interested in something? What catches your attention? You may realize that interest often comes from a story you heard. Stories engage us. When people tell stories, they want you to better understand their experiences. They hope hearing their story will trigger some type of response from you: admiration, astonishment, wonder, empathy, humor, sympathy, pride—some way to connect with them one-on-one. A great example of this is the Humans of New York social media posts, a photoblog and book of street portraits and interviews collected on the streets of New York City.[71] Each post is written to draw you into the person's life to learn something about them. There have been multiple spin-offs of this around the world—a sign they are onto something that resonates well with others.

---

71 Brandon Stanton, "Humans of New York-About," Humans of New York, accessed September 29, 2020.

In the ALS Ice Bucket Challenge, Pete Frates and others were able to use their stories to build a foundation of knowledge about ALS that others could support. Each post built a connection to someone else, maybe even someone you knew with ALS, and created a firestorm of empathy and care for those battling ALS.

How do you find stories? Well, this is where your staff, board, volunteers, and clients come in! Because of their interactions with your organization, they can be a great source for identifying possible stories. In an article for the *Stanford Social Innovation Review*, Julie Dixon said, "Regardless of whether the instigator of a nonprofit's storytelling culture comes from the bottom or the top, experts agree that the mindset of thinking and communicating in terms of stories must permeate throughout the organization to be successful."[72] Getting everyone on board with storytelling is best when you can ***create a guiding coalition of storytellers.*** The guiding coalition should be comprised of people across the organization that others know and trust. They share their experiences with others inside and outside the organization, and it helps build a strong base from which everyone feels empowered to share the organization's message through stories.

Julia Campbell, author of several nonprofit marketing and social media articles and books, outlined five ways to build a culture within your nonprofit that will help you identify stories. She noted, "All nonprofit professionals and volunteers need to start thinking of themselves as storytellers

---

72 Julie Dixon, "Building a Storytelling Culture," *Stanford Social Innovation Review*, October 27, 2014.

first, rather than simply Executive Directors, Development Directors, or Board Members. A comprehensive marketing and fundraising plan are of no use without good stories to fuel it."[73] So how can you do this?

DEVELOPING A CULTURE THAT EMBRACES STORYTELLING

Having a culture in which people within the organization feel safe and want to contribute is critical. No one wants to offer up ideas or take the risk of being called out for something they said if you haven't built a strong culture in which new ideas and thoughts are accepted. Campbell references that in order to gain buy-in, you need to make sure your board, staff, and volunteers understand why and how stories can benefit the nonprofit. What goals do you hope to achieve by sharing stories? Today, donors expect to hear stories; in fact, they want to hear them and know their donation made a difference.[74] As a donor to my university, hearing from a student that my scholarship donation meant they could focus on their studies just makes me want to give more! Campbell also points out that data is good, but a story can give deeper meaning to the data. Along the way, you may even pick up ideas you had not considered before!

Developing a culture of storytelling should empower your staff and volunteers and make them feel what they're doing really matters. Thanking and identifying them will go a long

---

73 Julia Campbell, "How to Create A Culture of Storytelling in Your Nonprofit," *CauseVox* (Blog). Accessed June 16, 2020.

74 Ibid.

way to strengthen the culture.[75] Campbell suggests a good way to get people to become more comfortable with looking for stories is to ***open each meeting or get-together with a story***. This allows people to hear stories from others and possibly relate them to their own future story ideas. If you make storytelling part of the agenda, over time contributors will be more willing to share stories. Using open-ended questions focusing on how the experience made the person feel will often lead to greater depth and content.

If you find your staff is still struggling with this, don't be afraid to hold a nonprofit storytelling workshop.[76] Sometimes bringing in an outside voice can help people get over a hurdle that may be holding them back. I equate this to parenting. We can make suggestions until we're blue in the face, but when someone different tells them the same thing, children will listen!

I know from my own experience of talking to clients, constituents, volunteers, and donors, along with my students, that many of them have a unique story to tell. All of us have a story inside; it is just waiting for the opportunity to be told.

Sandy Rees, nonprofit fundraising coach and trainer said, "Shared stories can tie whole cultures and groups together. Shared stories bind all sorts of people, from families to religious groups. Your best friend is your best friend because there are a few stories only the two of you share. In the nonprofit sector, stories are one of the strongest ways to

---

75 Ibid.

76 Ibid.

make emotional connections between donors and charities. Nonprofit storytelling lets donors and volunteers know that they are making an impact and making life better for real people."[77]

THE STORIES WE TELL: EXAMPLES IN ACTION

Eva Montibello, CEO of Alpha E Consulting in Haverhill, Massachusetts, shared how nonprofits could use storytelling in social media better. She said, "I think nonprofits are so mission-driven that they do one thing on social media and they think, 'Oh, okay we did it,' but not realizing that you've got to move that story to the next level."

Montibello told the story of how she was able to help a local nonprofit align its public relations with social media. "We started off initially with public relations by sending press releases. Next, we took the press release and sliced it up into little pieces and turned it into to social media posts. We would pull quotes and statistics out and convert them for social media posts. If you put out a whole press release on social media, everybody's going to read the first two lines and be done with it. Basically, what we did was we took the press release and reformatted it to social media. An example would be, using statistics, the nonprofit provided underwear to over 1,000 seniors and children in April. Another example is we would put a picture of the executive director up, or a picture of a piece of stock photography of children or seniors, and say, 'These are the people that we impacted.'"

77 Sandy Rees, "How You Can Use Nonprofit Storytelling to Increase Donations and Involvement." *Get Fully Funded.* June 18, 2019.

Montibello went on to share another social media campaign that provided new socks for people in need. "Look at how important it is to have dry socks. We all know that matters because you can make the story very personal; you know how it feels to be in soggy socks. Everybody knows that feeling and everyone hates that feeling. It resonates with the reader." Every post has to connect with the reader on an emotional level, and storytelling helps inform and educate the public in a very personal way, particularly if they can relate to it, as in the case of wet socks. *Find out what moves your audience because that is where your stories can be found.*

Colleen Gordon, social media manager at UMass Lowell, talked about working with a local quilt museum. "At the quilt museum, I'm trying to tell a story in a way where you get that feeling of a small museum; it's very intimate and it has really great exhibitions. I'm trying to help them tell a story through Instagram. You can do that in the stories feature. The curator and everybody that works there are all brilliant in what they do. My job is to help bring that to life in a story."

Gordon went on to describe how they can use storytelling to raise brand awareness. Gordon said, "They are trying to build awareness and let people know they exist because a lot of people don't know that they are here. There's such a big market in the quilting world. So, my goal is to raise brand awareness, let people know outside of Lowell or the surrounding towns that they exist and that they have amazing exhibitions. Building attendance and awareness is where I try and help them." Viewing their gallery on Instagram is a color explosion of quilts, and the number of posts and engagement from visitors from a larger geographical setting has allowed the organization to increase its base.

I asked Gordon if she had any advice for nonprofits, and here's what she said: "Really have a strategy before jumping on social media. I can't stress that enough, because a lot of times you get on there, and you start posting, and don't really have a message people can get on board with. That would be my advice to nonprofits or to anyone thinking about creating a social media presence anywhere."

Nonprofits need to tell stories. Storytelling allows us to connect with viewers and build a relationship with them. I asked Elizabeth Cannon, executive director of the Lowell Association for the Blind, if she had an example of a post that became a story, and she reminded me of a staff member's and her experience one summer day. Dorothy is a former English teacher who lost her sight at birth after receiving too much oxygen, which was commonly given without understanding the implications in premature infants. She is also an excellent pianist and singer and has filled her life with music and song whenever possible. A local bank, as part of its commitment to the arts in the downtown, had placed a piano on the main street for anyone to play. Many people would stop and play the piano, and kids especially loved it!

One day, Dorothy was waiting for the Road Runner (local transit service) to take her home. As usual, the service had given her a large window of time in which she could get picked up. Dorothy found herself sitting at the piano, encouraged by her friends and the staff of the Lowell Association for the Blind to play and sing for them.

As she sat there, she picked up her hands, found the keys, and began to play. Now, Dorothy didn't just sit calmly playing; she threw her whole self into the movement of the music. People stopped what they were doing and looked up, surprised to see the white cane Dorothy uses to navigate. Phone cameras begin rolling, as the audience realize a blind woman was playing completely by ear, without any sheet music.

As she continued to play for those who had gathered around her, a local photographer from the newspaper captured her performance. He reached out to find out more about her, and Elizabeth Cannon told him about Dorothy's life: her love of anything musical, her ability to teach people how to use Braille, and the inspiration she is for so many.

The story and photos were posted online by the nonprofit, which tagged the bank. When the bank shared it on its social media, the nonprofit was able to see how quickly that video was spread to others and gained a much wider audience than it could have on its own. This is also an example of the way for-profit businesses can help nonprofits—a partnering that benefits both organizations.

So, the big question is, "How do nonprofits make this happen more frequently?" How do we find the stories that should be told and use them to spread information and awareness of nonprofit organizations? This is where the social media coordinator can really help the nonprofit, by spending time to connect the stories of its clients, constituents, volunteers, and donors to communicate the value the nonprofit brings to the community, no matter what the size.

The stories we tell have the power to leverage momentum, and the current high use of videos to tell stories on Facebook and Instagram is providing additional ways viewers can relate what they see to their own lives.

MELANIE'S STORY CONTINUES—A DREAM REALIZED

"After my diagnosis in 2017, I went back to work, of course, and everything was just like usual. Nothing really changed with my health right away. I was fortunate enough that I was able to go to work each day and continue living our life, my husband's and mine, the way we had been.

"I had made plans that I was going to retire at fifty-nine and a half and at the time I was fifty-five. So I was a few years off from my intended plan. One thing I knew I wanted to do when I did retire was to move to the ocean in Maine. It was a plan that I had for many years. I actually had found the house I wanted to buy three years earlier, when visiting a friend in Maine. It was on the market, but at that time I had no intention of retiring. I was much too young to consider retiring, and we just didn't have the funds to own two homes. Fast forward to 2017. We were fortunate enough to learn that the house I loved three years earlier was for sale again.

"After looking into finances and trying to make it work, with the help of a relative, we were able to make an offer on the house in Maine. Our offer was accepted, everything worked out, and we bought the home in Ogunquit in September 2017.

"At that time, it was our second home; we still had our house in Chelmsford. I was still going to work each day; we would come up on the weekends and have friends visit. It's a mile from the ocean, and it's just a lovely community. We've met quite a few people here now that are really just great people. The aspect of the location—close to the beach—has just worked out very well. My husband has been able to buy a boat, and he keeps it not far from us, about four miles away. It was a dream of his to be able to own a boat near the ocean. So, I have to say, we've been lucky to be able to do this and I'm very grateful for it.

CHAPTER 9

EFFECTIVE USE OF SOCIAL MEDIA IN GOOD TIMES AND IN BAD TIMES

Every nonprofit, no matter what cause it serves, faces moments when it needs to get information out that is either exciting or difficult to address. Social media has provided a way to do this in real time, unlike with traditional channels of communication. However, the nonprofit must recognize that even though social media allows us to transmit information quickly, the nonprofit must be careful about what it says, just as if they were sending a letter or newsletter to share the information. More than one nonprofit has found itself in a difficult place with messaging that was not ready for prime time.

Writer and storyteller Andrew Friedenthal wrote, "In 2012, the Susan G. Komen Breast Cancer Foundation chose to cut off funding to Planned Parenthood because of political pressure. It faced a social media uproar in response, and though it reversed its decision after only three days, the damage to its image, its organization, and its bottom line was permanent. Because it was unable to readily respond to such a social media backlash, the following fiscal year it lost, according to a Los Angeles Times report, '$77 million, or fully 22 percent of the foundation's income.' Though giant nonprofits such as the Susan G. Komen foundation may be able to weather these storms and losses, a similar type of backlash could spell the end of your own, smaller nonprofit."[78] In fact, I would argue it is doubly important that the nonprofit's messaging be clear and succinct because as everyone knows, on the internet things exist forever.

Let's take a look at how to share good news on social media.

THE GOOD NEWS WAGON

You would think wanting to share good news about your organization would be easy, but in reality, there may be reasons why you're reluctant to put information out there on social media. Sometimes staff or board members are wary of sharing good news because they are concerned that if you say you're doing your job well, people will stop helping. For example, did your fundraising meet a milestone goal? This seems an obvious time to share this success with the world. Often there are concerns that "if the public sees we're doing well on this, they won't see the need or feel the urgency to

78 Andrew Friedenthal, "What's Your Nonprofit Social Media Crisis Response Plan?" Software Advice, May 16, 2018.

give." Put in those terms, you can see why there may be reluctance in sharing good news. However, highlighting what you've accomplished and including an urge to help reach your final goal and beyond is better than not sharing the information.

I recently saw a Facebook post about raising money for a local food pantry during the COVID-19 pandemic. The creator of the post, someone well-known in the community, shared the milestones as they were met every few days. Near the end, when she was just a few hundred dollars short, she added a new post urging those who could to give "just a little bit more" so the organization could doubly benefit from a newly announced matching pledge. This announcement created even more excitement, and that day she surpassed her original goal *and* was able to announce that the pledge would now provide twice as many meals as it could before! This is a great example of utilizing social media to reach your goals by creating excitement and a "buzz" to cause a sensation and get people talking about it and sharing it via social media. Posting lets your publics know what you are doing to help those you serve.

As the ALS Ice Bucket Challenge was exploding with popularity, ALSA realized it had to keep the public fully informed. In our interview, Carrie Munk stated, "I think a lot of nonprofit organizations have crisis plans, but it's usually as it relates to a disaster or, for example, the global pandemic. Crisis planning is not necessarily the good kind, like what were to happen if our cause takes off? There is this unprecedented level of giving that we've never experienced before. How would we step up? How would we repurpose existing staff? What things are essential to our business that we have to keep doing? It's those kinds of plans that I think every charity should be ready to handle and that's what really stood out to me."

Another example of sharing good news: the nonprofit showcases its volunteers and the work they contribute to the organization. If the nonprofit's social media post doesn't include a call for new volunteers to join them, some people may think the organization already has plenty of volunteers and doesn't need any more. You want to include wording and a link inviting others to join in to be part of helping solve the problem the nonprofit is addressing. The nonprofit utilizing social media must understand the implications of each and every post and take great care when making them. Each post should engage the reader and serve to inform, educate, and act.

THE OTHER SIDE

At some point in its life, every nonprofit is going to have to manage a social media post that is not a good reflection on the organization. Examples of this range from the very serious—implications about volunteers, staff, or board members, misuse of funds raised, workplace harassment, and workplace conditions—to less serious—misstatements, errors, or omissions. How your organization manages these situations makes a huge difference in how the public views and trusts your nonprofit.

In the digital age, the public can quickly gain information from online news and television, and we're seeing further reliance on social media as a news source. This means people are more likely to have easy access to ways to express themselves quickly and publicly via social media, and sometimes, without thinking about the implications of their posts. In addition, because people have become accustomed to using their phones for everything, even the best intentions can go astray quickly.

In 2011, an employee of the American Red Cross thought she was posting to her own account and posted about a friend finding eight beers on the American Red Cross feed instead. Luckily, a social media director, Wendy Harmon, found it quickly and deleted the post, tweeting a humorous response about confiscating the keys.[79] This was a terrific example of good crisis management that removed the inappropriate social media and found a way to turn it into an educational and positive response to the situation.

SOCIAL MEDIA CRISIS MANAGEMENT

Every organization, for-profit or nonprofit, should have a crisis management plan in place, but often, particularly for smaller nonprofits, this can be challenging to keep updated. The best practice for a nonprofit would be to review its crisis management plan yearly with the board of directors and staff members. In addition, social media guidelines should be provided in all information given to board members, staff, and volunteers. It should also identify for everyone the difference between a social media crisis and a social media issue. This

79 Katie Leimkuehler. "The Red Cross Rogue Tweet: How to Turn a Social Media Mistake into a Positive Outcome," *CPrime,* November 22, 2016.

way there will be few questions raised about how to address the concern promptly.

Crisis management strategist Melissa Agnes said, "If you can answer 'yes' to any of the following questions, it's highly likely that you can consider your brand in a social media crisis—and it's time to activate your crisis communications plan.

- Is there, or is there the potential to be, a strong negative emotional impact?
- Does the issue or situation fall under your brand's pre-determined categories of crisis situations?
- Is the situation, or is there potential for the situation to go viral?
- May this situation result in potential reputational damage to your brand?"[80]

I particularly like that Agnes walks you through the questions to ask to determine your response. Crises require careful and deliberate responses that may include legal and additional support.

Agnes also discussed categories she considers to be social media issues—of concern to the organization, but not at the level of a crisis. Social media issues could be rumors, negative or unacceptable comments, miscommunications, or service issues.[81] Determining whether you're dealing with an issue or a crisis is important in how the organization will respond.

---

80 Melissa Agnes, "Detecting A Social Media Crisis vs. A Social Media Issue," September 26, 2012.

81 Ibid.

Below is an example of an experience regarding a nonprofit organization and an employee's social media use.

On opening my Facebook feed one day, the first item was a post by a former employee of a nonprofit. It showed a picture of the former employee and a current employee getting together for dinner. In the post, the former employee alluded to "stories to tell" that did not actually state anything negative but may have been perceived as a negative comment about the organization. I quickly took a screenshot and sent it to the board president and the executive director. They determined a review of social media use by current employees should be conducted and reminded the staff of the importance of being aware of the content of posts they are tagged in.

This was really a minor incident, and it was not the fault of the current employee, but it served as a catalyst for a review of the social media policy of the organization, which is always a good thing. Becoming comfortable and complacent with the way things are done is so easy, and this incident served as a reminder of the need for ongoing training and instruction as social media continues to garner a larger share of our online attention.

KEY ELEMENTS OF A SOCIAL MEDIA CRISIS MANAGEMENT PLAN

The experience from the situation described above highlights one of the first things you should think about when responding to a social media crisis or issue:

Who will speak for the organization?

In many cases, the executive director or the president of the board of directors will speak for the organization, but everyone should know automatically who that person is and make sure that whoever is chosen is someone who can speak for the organization well. Not everyone is comfortable in becoming the public face of the nonprofit. Recognize that the spokesperson must represent the organization in a professional and calm manner. Every member of the staff and board should know to refer all questions and comments from media, donors, and the community to the spokesperson and not attempt to address the questions themselves. Social media issues and crises call for a clear and concise message from the organization spokesperson.

The second thing you want to keep in mind:

> *The spokesperson and the organization must act in a transparent and honest manner.*

If you made a mistake, don't try to blame someone else. If you try to cover it up, you will be found out; it is only a matter of time. People understand that mistakes happen, and by turning a mistake into an opportunity to improve what you were doing, you may be able to deflect some of the negativity surrounding the issue. This leads to the next item:

> *If you made a mistake, apologize.*

In a timely manner, account for what you did, and tell the public how you will fix it. This is a way to reduce the impact of the issue and the damage to your nonprofit's brand.[82]

There are several templates available online for developing a crisis plan that includes a social media crisis plan. I encourage you to find one that best fits the needs of your nonprofit and have included some links in the Appendix to help you. Though you may think this a wasted effort, I can assure you that when a situation arises, you will be very glad you have made a plan for addressing it!

82 Beth Kanter, "Two Examples of Nonprofit Social Media That Will Make You Smile (and learn a best practice or two)," October 4, 2017.

CHAPTER 10

PUTTING YOUR STRATEGY INTO ACTION

So, you've come this far. What to do next? How do you find a way to market your organization through purposeful goals with posts that lead to the achievement of those goals? Recently I had a student who was working on a social media project for a local historical society. He had good ideas, but he just didn't know how to put them to work for the organization. He was too wrapped up in thinking that posting *more* was the goal. Please don't make this mistake! More is not better if it doesn't help you achieve what you want your marketing to do. **"'More Posts' Is Not a Strategy" #MPINS.**

FIRST STEP: BUILDING UNDERSTANDING OF THE NEED OF A GOAL

Sit down with your team and determine what you want as an outcome. What is your goal? I strongly suggest you do this as part of a group effort, and there are two reasons why. One is that getting everyone involved can increase your team cohesion and help people feel like part of the solution. Think about this: someone comes to you with an already developed plan to do something, and you can immediately see holes in it. You feel like they didn't value your input, and you are not as likely to be fully on board with implementing it. To prevent this from happening, make sure to approach information gathering as a team activity. The other stakeholders will have great ideas to develop and build on. The second reason is actually part of the first reason: you alone cannot possibly know all the different viewpoints for the goal. This can be hard for some who don't like to give up control, but I guarantee you will end with better results if you can build support among your team members. Remember, your staff and board are your best marketers, and if they aren't, they should be. This is why being inclusive is important.

When you meet with your team, I suggest you not try to do everything at once. As a reminder, one of the differences between for-profit and nonprofit businesses is that for-profit businesses have customers, *but nonprofits have four different groups of customers: clients, constituents, volunteers, and donors.* Each of these "publics" have different needs, though there is occasionally some overlap.

Here's an example: say you have determined you want to gain more donors. After all, doesn't every nonprofit want this? Yes! But you need to think about it even further. Are you looking to gain new donors who have never given to the organization before? They have similar, but different needs than existing donors. A new donor needs to trust you to do what you say you will do with their donation. They want to know what you will do, who it is helping, and why it is helping. Your job is to educate them. If they are already donors, you need to consider posts that will encourage them to donate again. A great way to do this is to show them what you have done with past donations and how they have helped the nonprofit complete its mission.

Uncommon Threads in Lawrence, Massachusetts, is an exemplar in maximizing their impact through social media. They provide clothing for women who are socioeconomically challenged as a way to empower their clients. The organization offers complete outfits to women who need proper clothing for an interview, a new job, or just a boost of self-confidence that comes from looking and feeling great! The nonprofit provides individual appointments for styling and covers everything clients need, from proper undergarments to outerwear to accessories.

Why would someone want to donate to the organization? Maybe a sense of helping others, giving back because someone helped them, they know you or some of your staff, they've heard about you from friends, or they just like the idea of helping women feel better about themselves. What kind of message will resonate? Uncommon Threads uses the power of social media through storytelling. They ask the clients to describe how dressing well makes them feel. They include pictures and short videos that showcase just how great the client looks and feels after being styled. They have the volunteer stylist explain why they volunteer their services and what it means to them. Storytelling is a great way for people to build a connection with an organization because they can hear, read, and see the difference it can make.

Make sure to include a Donate button or a link to your website so that people who are moved to donate can do it immediately, not later when they've often forgotten about it. Immediacy is everything here! Respond promptly, within twenty-four hours, thanking them for their donation. A thank you goes a long way in building a relationship with anyone. It lets them know you value their contribution and want them to know how much they are appreciated.

SECOND STEP: SET A SCHEDULE

Now that you've determined your goal, what are some ways your team thinks will best get the message to the public? Again, this is important: rely on your team! Make them a part of the decision-making process and they will be more likely to embrace the idea of social media that *works* for your nonprofit. In doing this exercise on a monthly basis, you will help them to start identifying moments with your publics that they themselves could capture. Photos? Videos? Stories? A combination? If they understand the goals you are trying to achieve and the profile of the target segment, they will help you get there. People don't work for or become involved in nonprofits if they don't care about the people they are serving. Everyone is a contributor!

I strongly recommend not trying to hit every segment at once, at least initially. Here's where *implementing a content calendar will help you.* I introduced these in Chapter 7 but wanted to provide you a reminder here. A content calendar allows you to design, develop, and schedule your posts all in one location. Free content calendars are easily available online and will help you organize your posts.

You can designate different times of the month and year when you want to focus on a specific group. If you try to make sure you have posts that are relevant to every public all the time, setting goals that you can achieve and measure will be more challenging. In nonprofit organizations, there is often overlap between groups, too. You may have a donor who is a volunteer or a client who is a donor. People who already care about your organization will probably feel a connection to many posts. Still, identifying *why* you are using social media and *what* you want to accomplish to reach your goal is important. I cannot emphasize this enough!

THIRD STEP: BE CREATIVE!

Now that you have your goals and have received input from others, you have the chance to be creative! This is the fun part! You should have a list of suggestions for posts that are grouped around each public. I encourage you to think of each group separately. Based on your desired goal, develop a series of posts that build toward that goal and use a social media content calendar to organize them. For the previous example of attracting new donors, you want to send a consistent message of the needs of your organization. Do you have a new or existing program that you are looking to fund? How can you visually send that message? What wording do you need to include that encourages people to learn more? Engage your readers in a conversation with you, through commenting and polls. Interaction is key!

Remember, you do not have to reinvent the wheel. Make learning about how other nonprofits utilize their social media a priority. Check out their social media posts and make note of things they do well and things you would want to improve. How can you take the information you learn and make it work for your organization? A great exercise is to ask your staff and board to find good and bad examples to share during a meeting. This helps people to really think about what makes a good post and how they can help the nonprofit improve.

FOURTH STEP: ENGAGE! THE *MOST* IMPORTANT PIECE OF ADVICE

Once you've begun posting, make sure you are tracking the results. Both Facebook and Instagram provide analytics that help you, and they are continually updating and making improvements to their analytics. I'm not going to tell you about specific analytics because you need to be familiar with their analytics available when you are reading this. Social media analytics tools are always being added, updated, and improved. What I am going to talk to you about is the importance of engaging with your social media responders.

Engagement may be the most important piece of advice I can give you. Make certain you are doing this! It seems simple, but I know from personal experience posting on nonprofits' websites that it is not done well. You need to respond to every post or request, always and promptly. The maximum amount of time that should pass before responding should be no more than twenty-four hours, and ideally, within two to four hours, seven days a week and holidays. Social media doesn't sleep! This means you will have to be checking on your posts at least twice a day. Thanking people should become an integral part of your social media campaign, along with encouraging them to share your post with their network.

This is partly what made the ALS Ice Bucket Challenge successful in the first days and weeks and contributed to its going viral. Pete Frates involved everyone on Team Frate Train by communicating through his eye gazer. "'Quick, get on your computers and start liking and sharing every one of these videos you see on our Team Frate Train home page on Facebook.' Pete ordered. 'Comment on everything. Please say, 'Thank you. Thank you for joining us in this fight.'"[83] This was the moment he had been waiting for—a chance to take their ALS awareness and fundraising campaign to a new level.

Engagement is about encouraging people to learn more about your nonprofit, the people it serves, and the programs and services you offer.

A post shared by a friend might be what alerts someone of your organization's existence. I have learned of friends' nonprofit interests through social media. For example, I recently saw a post for a friend's organization I had given to in the past. Due to the COVID-19 pandemic, many nonprofits are unable to hold fundraisers. However, utilizing Facebook, they are getting the message out that even though the pandemic is precluding them from hosting an on-site fundraiser, they still need to raise money for their cause. That is exactly what caught my eye, especially since it is an organization to which

83 Casey Sherman and Dave Wedge, *The Ice Bucket Challenge: Pete Frates and the Fight against ALS*, (Lebanon, NH: University Press of New England, 2017), 111-112.

I typically make a donation. When I saw the post, it served as a reminder that even though they aren't hosting an event this year, I can still donate. It was their past engagement with me via social media that drove me to donate again.

Don't underestimate the power of engaging with your publics. How you make them feel when you respond to their interactions with your nonprofit's posts will leave a long-lasting impression.

MELANIE'S STORY CONTINUES: LEAVING WORK

"Life continued along. Now we could go to Ogunquit on the weekends, not just if I had time off. My husband, Alan, was still working at the music store, but in December of 2017, he had complications. Due to his illness, we found ourselves back and forth to Lahey Clinic again. I was working and making sure he was all set.

"My work was going fine, I was able, physically, to continue to work. I was still in pretty good shape. I was able to climb three flights of stairs without any thought at all. But it began to catch up with me. You know, going to work in the morning and going up those stairs means you have to go back down. If I need to see somebody in their office, I might have to climb two flights of stairs. It had never been a problem for me, other than feeling winded sometimes. I felt like it was a good way to keep moving around, but in January 2018, I really started to feel fatigued.

"I also started to feel the emotional piece of my diagnosis. I went to work every day. You think it's going to keep your mind busy, which it did. I had plenty to do, people to see, and many projects going on, but emotionally, it would just stop me in the middle of the day. I'd have to go in my office, shut the door, and just have a little mini breakdown in there, because I didn't want people to see me upset. That was happening more and more, and I was just feeling the exhaustion. It was winter, so I was cold, of course, and that didn't help.

"I was feeling overwhelmed; everything was starting to take its toll. So, I had a conversation, in passing, with Maura Sweeney, senior vice president/chief human resources officer at the bank. Maura has been a very good friend of mine for years. I would share with her how I was doing. She was a very good shoulder to lean on all the time, but especially now, and she listened to what I had to say about how tired I was. On top of all of this, Al was not feeling well and having complications. It was just a lot.

"In January I sat down and had a meeting with Maura and the president of the bank. They had been there thirty-six years. They knew me very well, and they knew what was going on; I didn't keep my diagnosis a secret. They had the attitude of 'You have to find a way to live your life now, while you're still fairly healthy and able to do things.' With the exhaustion I was feeling, I didn't want to give less than I've always given. That takes a toll, also. It was decided at that time that it was probably best that I start by going out on disability. Staying wasn't going to do me any good; it was going to probably exacerbate my condition. I was exhausted most of the time; it was just time. They were very supportive; I can't say enough about how great they were to me. There was just positive support from the time I was diagnosed until I left and beyond. They were very good to me.

"So, my last day of work ended up being January 19, 2018. I have to say, not having to get up every day, go to work, and do the things that needed to be done was a big relief of the stress I had been under. It wasn't an easy decision to make, when you've been somewhere that long, and you had plans to work for at least another four years. It was just a big change."

CHAPTER 11

LESSONS LEARNED

LEARNING FROM EXPERIENCE—ALS ICE BUCKET CHALLENGE

Have you ever wondered what happened after the success of the 2014 ALS Ice Bucket Challenge? What was learned from this experience? What worked and what didn't work? Did they learn things that would help all nonprofits do better in the future? This last chapter explores the lessons learned from some of the people directly involved with ALSA.

THE IMPORTANCE OF REFLECTION

We can all learn from past experience with events. In fact, something I strongly recommend is a debriefing session following any nonprofit event. Don't let a lot of time pass between the event and asking for feedback. You should query your board members, staff, volunteers, and even some of your guests. I've gotten some of my best responses when, the day following the event, I've sent out a request for suggestions for the future. The event is fresh in participant's minds, so they are less likely to forget. Often, these are small things, like making sure we have a smooth system for checking out following a silent auction or ensuring that the program starts on time. I also recommend checking in with people a second time, maybe when a couple of weeks or a month have passed. You'd be surprised what people think of when they've had a chance to step back and reflect.

Based on her experience with the ALS Ice Bucket Challenge, I asked Carrie Munk, chief marketing and communications officer for ALSA, if she had any words of advice on how to engage donors and keep people interested. Munk noted, "People, generally, like to feel part of something bigger than themselves. In 2015, we wanted to create a sense of nostalgia. We wanted people to pause and remember how fun and exciting it was to be part of the ALS Ice Bucket Challenge the previous year. From a communications perspective, we created tools like infographics and videos to help tap into that nostalgia. We also aggressively reported on research progress, which resulted in headlines in major media outlets right at the one-year anniversary mark. Ultimately, we knew that not every donor would do the challenge again the following year. But our development team, using the data we accumulated, really made an effort to figure out where the best opportunities for giving were."

This highlights one of the important takeaways from the book: have a strategy! Remember, social media is just one part of marketing for the whole organization. How can it contribute to the goals you have set for your organizational strategy?

TRANSPARENCY

No matter how you raise money, being transparent to your publics and letting them know how much you've raised and how you are spending it are important. Nothing makes the public angrier than finding out you are not spending the money raised on what you said you would do with it.

In June 2020, the Minnesota Freedom Fund (MFF), an organization whose mission is to eliminate cash bail in Minnesota while providing bail until this is accomplished, raised over $30 million! This success was due in large part to the awareness raised by George Floyd's death. In the two years prior, the MFF had only raised $160,000, so you can imagine that this giant influx of funding brought concerns, too. There was only one full-time paid staff member at the time! The board had to decide what to do with the funding and knew they had to keep the public informed, too. This decision included asking donors to donate to other nonprofits serving Minnesota.[84] The board knew they needed to keep donors informed of their plans or risk alienating people from giving in the future.

This will make an interesting case study or book in the future. The MFF only had a small board of seven directors who had to start meeting almost every day to address the questions of the media and public. To go from "zero to sixty" meant a major change in how the organization was operating.[85]

---

84 Mark Hrywna, "Unrest Spurs $30 Million To Minnesota Freedom Fund," *The Nonprofit Times*, June 8, 2020.

85 Ibid.

How well it succeeds will provide lessons to nonprofits for the future.

Making sure they kept the public aware of how their contributions were helping was a major part of responding to the ALS Ice Bucket Challenge. Carrie Munk stated, "In the nonprofit world, no one reports out daily how much money you're bringing in during a crisis; it's just not done. Once you hit a milestone, it's okay to do this. For example, it's been six months and we'd announce we've raised X amount of dollars, but organizations typically don't ever report out on daily fundraising figures. I made the decision pretty early on, with the support of our CEO, to report each day's total. I was getting calls from journalists, every day, saying, 'How much money did you bring in today?'"

In the meantime, according to Munk, "Big Bird [Sesame Street], Ronald McDonald, and Bill Gates were releasing their ice bucket challenge videos on social media. Traditional media were using those clips in their broadcasts and reporting on how much money was being raised at the time. So, the media strategy helped fuel the social media strategy, because it just created more content for social media. There were these nontraditional stories that $5 million was raised today, so we would put the fundraising figure on the website every day. It must have been two months we reported every single day. It just added fuel to the media coverage, which I don't think we would have had otherwise."

Munk went on to say, "I thought that was interesting, too, because sometimes people, when they think about disasters in other parts of the world where the Red Cross raises money, you'd never hear about how the money was spent. In traditional times of fundraising, you want to be very careful with what you report back to people and corporations. We just made the decision. Let's look at our balance and we can see how many online donations were processed. This might be a little bit messy, and we can reconcile at the end. People were desperate to know how much money was being raised. People thought, 'Oh well, people are doing this, but they're not really giving, they're just doing their videos.' So, in all my media interviews, I would respond, 'Actually, we brought in $3 million yesterday. Yes, people are giving.'"

As head of creative at ALSA, Brian Frederick echoed this need for transparency, too. He said, "One thing I did learn, and I think was really important and critical to what we did, was I always wanted to be as transparent as possible about what we were doing. I kept emphasizing this isn't like a $115 million bequest that we received, or a gift from a major donor. This was 2.5 million people, basically the larger public as a whole, who donated to us and have an investment or have a stake in this. It's up to us to be transparent about how we're spending the money, how it's making a difference. Tell that story proactively, rather than having somebody else write that story for us. Early on, I really pushed for having a separate page on our website where all the grants that we had given as a result of this would be listed. You could click on them and there were descriptions and a pie chart, in the form of a bucket, that showed exactly how much money was raised and how that money was being apportioned by mission area."

This transparency helped increase the momentum of the ALS Ice Bucket Challenge because people could see and hear in the media that the money being raised would be used to fight ALS through research and support of ALS patients. Their contribution was making a difference. When donors feel they have helped, they want to give more. Here, they were able to further the challenge by sharing it on social media, which again led donors and volunteers to feel they were part of something important.

LOOKING FORWARD

Perhaps one of the harder things to do in nonprofit organizations is to find a repeatable event that people will pay to do again. Most nonprofits do develop some type of signature event that they become known for producing, but is it possible to do this when you've had unbridled success, such as the ALS Ice Bucket Challenge or the Minnesota Freedom Fund? I asked Brian Frederick what he thought.

"I think early on, for me, I was very much concerned with what happens next. Where does this go? How do we leverage this, and keep the momentum going? I remember at the time there were some staffers who were really burned out, because of all of that had happened. This was understandable. I, as an outsider, a consultant and somebody just coming into the organization was puzzled, because I was thinking, 'Here's the biggest thing that ever happened to your organization and you should be thrilled and taking advantage of this and doing everything you can.' In my mind, I always saw this as an incredible opportunity and wanted people to step up to try and help keep the momentum."

This is important to keep in mind—the excitement can be amazing, but it can be very draining. Over a six- to eight-week period, people were working 24/7 just trying to keep the movement at the forefront of the public eye. That can be exhausting. As a nonprofit leader, you have to find ways to allow time for rest and encourage your employees to decompress while still keeping the campaign in the media.

Frederick acknowledged this challenge and stated, "That became my focus. Very early on the thinking was, 'Well, what happens next year, how do we keep this going, what do we ask people to do?' So much of my communication work was what should those early messages be? I remember I had a conversation with a corporate development person. They had a similar feeling of, 'You now have thousands of companies who have done this ALS Ice Bucket Challenge, so how do you continue to engage them? How do you continue to reach them?' I think that it has probably been the hardest question I have ever faced in my career."

If you followed the ALS Ice Bucket Challenge, you probably wondered why you really haven't heard much about it again. Frederick stated, "What do you do with the most amazing social media phenomenon and how do you keep it going? I don't know that I have a particularly good answer. I have a sense of what maybe doesn't work. It's a matter of expectations versus reality. But, you know, we had 17 million people upload videos. I think 2.5 million people of those have donated. And then, five hundred thousand of those opted to let us continue to communicate with them. A number of people who took the challenge didn't have any interest in ALS. If you don't have a connection to ALS, you just kind of lose interest in the cause. My goal, since I've started there, has always been to give people who don't have a connection with ALS a chance to care about ALS. How do we get that wider audience, who doesn't know one of the twenty thousand people at any given time that have ALS to care about this disease?"

CAN THEIR SUCCESS BE REPEATED?

Frederick raised an important question. Is the right choice to continue with the same type of event? Knowing how to proceed can be hard when something so powerful has become a part of your brand. Many organizations have been successful in repeating major events, but never one that became comparably viral via social media. Examples of organizations that hold successful yearly events include the Pan-Mass Challenge, which raises money for Dana Farber Cancer Institute, and the Susan G. Komen 3-Day walk to raise money for breast cancer research. Although these are large fundraisers raising millions of dollars, going viral on social media was not how they became a brand. Going viral is an elusive phenomenon that differentiates the ALS Ice Bucket Challenge from other nonprofit fundraising events.

Brian Frederick shared his experience. He said, "The biggest challenge with the Ice Bucket Challenge, no pun intended, is the framing is so literal that it makes it hard to get away from that framing. When we were trying to figure out what to do next, over the course of many months, we had conversations with several Madison Avenue executives who were connected to ALS—David Lubars, chairman/chief creative officer at BBDO; Tom Carroll, former CEO of TBWA, who lost his father to ALS; and Scott Kauffman, former chairman and CEO of MDC Partners, whose son has ALS. We kept coming back to it because everybody would say, 'Oh, you should try this next year, you should do this.' Obviously, after that success, every charity tried to come up with their own challenge. The Ice Bucket Challenge brand was the ALS Association, and to move away from that wouldn't have been really wrong, true. But if you have just the ALS Ice Bucket Challenge, well, there's not much else to do. We were talking with the head of creative at Facebook, and eventually it just came down to we have to do the Ice Bucket Challenge again; you have to get people to keep doing the Ice Bucket Challenge.

"Looking back, I think I would have probably tried to figure out something else or find a way that people could continue to do it but not expect it to be the worldwide phenomenon that it was. Could we make it so that before or sometime during every baseball game there's a challenge? I started the challenge idea that summer. Are there other ways to keep it going without having to be a social media thing? I think a few of our chapters have still managed to do that. They get local business leaders and CEOs and raise a bunch of money, so it's still happening a little bit in some of our communities. Maybe we should have pushed more for this to be a grassroots thing."

Frederick raised some interesting questions, but the success of the 2014 ALS Ice Bucket Challenge raises hope for so many. In 2019, ALSA reported that in the last five years, it has contributed $90 million to advancing research, resulting in the identification of five new genes related to ALS. The funds raised facilitated an increase in scientific collaboration and grew the number of clinical treatment centers from one hundred in 2014 to 156 today.[86] Without the ALS Ice Bucket Challenge, none of this would be possible. ***This is the power of social media.***

REFLECTING

The ALS Ice Bucket Challenge changed the way nonprofits think about using social media. Gone are the days when a few sporadic posts on social media can be considered marketing. The tremendous success of the ALS Ice Bucket Challenge, both in raising awareness and money, should make every nonprofit sit up and take notice. What is important is that nonprofits understand and recognize the power social media has on its publics.

The work done by ALSA in laying the groundwork for future fundraising efforts by nonprofit organizations should not be underestimated. Their ability early on to recognize and strategically use multiple forms of marketing provides nonprofits with a blueprint of how to grow their social media following through engagement, transparency, and communication.

The nonprofit sector has much to be thankful for due to the immense amount of publicity the ALS Ice Bucket Challenge raised for not just ALS, but all nonprofits. It was a call to action for nonprofits to recognize the importance of utilizing social media to reach the public. After the ALS Ice Bucket Challenge, every nonprofit realized it could maximize

86 "Ice Bucket Challenge dramatically accelerated the fight against ALS," ALS Association, Press Release, June 4, 2019.

social media tools to reach its publics. The opportunities are there. With a firm eye on the mission and a strategic marketing approach, social media can be the tool that helps nonprofits continue to educate, inform, and raise funds for their organization.

CONCLUSION

We began this journey discussing the ALS Ice Bucket Challenge of 2014. Remember? That was a call to action to pour a bucket of ice cold water over your head to raise awareness and funds for ALS. Who would have imagined that challenge would raise $115 million for ALSA!

That event made me wonder how other nonprofits could link social media to their overall marketing strategy. So the journey continued—winding its way through nonprofits, charity, philanthropy, the ALS Ice Bucket Challenge, and to my friend, Melanie, and her story of strength and determination. Hopefully, Melanie's story provided personal insight into the struggles people with diseases have to face every day. I hope it has kept your interest and provided you with knowledge, information, and a desire to help nonprofits improve their use of social media to further their cause.

Without nonprofits, the support and development of research would not be possible. But curing diseases is only one segment of the nonprofit sector. Nonprofits, as you learned, are everywhere. They're doing good work in fields such as education, culture, health, science, disabilities, sports—and so many more. As a society, we rely on the work of nonprofits to address the problems so many people face.

Social media can bring awareness, education, and support to any issue, and I wanted this book to reach people in a format that connects with the heart, not just the head. By laying the groundwork of the history of nonprofits, the importance of charity and philanthropy, and the changing climate for nonprofits in terms of government, I hope you come away with a better understanding of the value of nonprofits to society.

Charity has become integrated into American culture and the business environment in ways no other countries on Earth have utilized. The rise in the importance of corporate social responsibility has led to new ways of thinking. Smart and savvy philanthropic donors have discovered that if we want to solve big problems, we need to recognize that change takes innovation and large sums of money, along with a strategic way of implementing programs.

The rise of social media, such that it has become an integral part of everyday life, offers opportunities for nonprofits to leverage the assets they have through social media. This includes investing in expertise, applying strategic thinking, and integrating social media into your overall marketing strategy. Nonprofits that approach social media keeping this in mind will be able to end the struggle of feeling they are not posting often enough. Instead, they will recognize that **"'More Posts' Is Not a Strategy" #MPINS** and develop a social media plan that aligns with their mission and goals.

So remember, have a strategy! Social media is just one part of marketing the whole organization.

The ALS Ice Bucket Challenge has taught us that by understanding the nature of social media, the call to action it can create, and the ability to keep and engage viewers can lead to success. Nowhere is this clearer than in the prompt to call out three friends to take the ALS Ice Bucket Challenge and then share your video and ask them to do the same. That tactic, along with capturing videos of those participating, and the actual anticipation of what it might be like to be covered in icy water, provided the spark that set off a viral campaign. Now take that formula and apply it to your nonprofit. Will it be the next phenomenon? We don't know yet, but it will help ensure you are thinking strategically about what you post on social media.

It's worth repeating. A major take-away from this book is the need to develop a social media plan that is integrated with a marketing plan. Both need to align with the mission and goals of your organization and the strategy you will use to accomplish those goals. This level of understanding, along with recognizing the importance of including your staff and volunteers in identifying potential stories, will contribute to your success. They will help you identify those opportunities that can be expanded upon to show the work your nonprofit does for the community and beyond. Getting them on board includes helping them understand their role as marketers within the organization. To that end, I've developed two posters, The Power of Social Media and You Are a Marketer, to display in a common area frequented by staff and volunteers. I believe these will help staff and volunteers learn how to identify potential client, constituent, volunteer, and donor stories and encourage them to be part of the movement of "How to Tell Your Why." A color version of these can be found at

https://wakeupcall.finchfamily.org/PowerOfSocialMedia.pdf and https://wakeupcall.finchfamily.org/YouAreAMarketer.pdf.

We also discussed how to utilize social media in both good times and bad, because I think it is important to have a plan that can be quickly activated when needed. Being flexible when things are going well is important, and always "keep the door open" to allow for more donations: a challenge, invitation, matching funds. Never miss the opportunity to engage more fully with your audience.

We learned some lessons along this journey, too. Sometimes bad things happen to good people. Your post can cause a negative reaction due to things beyond your control. Take ownership, act quickly, and move on. People will remember you addressed it in a timely manner and didn't play the blame game. That will earn your organization respect and a loyal following.

I provided you with step-by-step instructions to put your action plan to work and offered examples of how you can facilitate this. You can do it! It takes drive and focus, but you can help your nonprofit improve its marketing by understanding the big picture *and* committing to a process that ensures you reach your goals.

By looking at the lessons learned from the ALS Ice Bucket Challenge, you gain the benefit of hindsight, which is always helpful. Doing a debrief following any type of event will help your nonprofit learn how to be better the next time. We can always learn! Use the information you gain to improve.

My goal for writing this book was to provide you with the skills, knowledge, and ability to help nonprofits utilize social media marketing to increase awareness for their cause and increase sustainable donations. With a strategic mindset, you can bring attention, education, and funding to your organization in a way that excites and motivates your followers to become involved. This engagement will bring energy and enthusiasm to your nonprofit. What's the end result, you ask? To provide continued services to your clients that help you meet your mission. At the end of the day, isn't that what all nonprofits want to do?

EPILOGUE

MELANIE'S STORY: WHAT A DIFFERENCE A DIAGNOSIS MAKES

"Prior to my diagnosis in 2017, I had a fairly active life. My husband and I enjoyed going to concerts, traveling, and socializing; we always had something going on. We enjoyed getting together with friends and family on the weekends. We took cruises with friends. We went to Aruba a few times and enjoyed that. Even though my husband had medical issues, we would plow through those and we would still stay very active. For exercise, I enjoyed walking; that was one of my favorite activities. My friend MaryRose and I would walk three miles at lunchtime, and I would come home at night and I would walk with my neighbors, Eileen and Jody. I belonged to a gym for exercise classes and yoga. Before my diagnosis, I could climb three flights of stairs at work without a problem.

"I would work all day and sometimes I'd attend charitable events at night. I always enjoyed a good social party. A lot of times I'd be the last person at the party, one of the last people to go home. It was always fun, and I really enjoyed being with people.

"After my diagnosis in 2017, things remained the same for a short period of time. My symptoms were mild, though I still had the problem with my right hand. It was starting to not function properly, and it was becoming weaker. I was still walking, no problem. And then, shortly after the summer, I began to stumble now and again. As time went on, the stumbling got worse. I started using a walker. Then, in 2018, I was planning to go on a cruise with my friends MaryRose, Tina, and Mike. I knew I needed something more than a walker. On a cruise there is a lot of walking traveling, so I purchased a portable electric wheelchair that folded up nicely and could go anywhere. It would take me to the plane, and then they would put it down in baggage and it would be there when I landed. That worked out well. We actually named 'her' Carrie, because she carried me! From there, she went on many trips; I have stickers all over her showing all the places she has been with me.

"Early on, my doctor told me not to rush to get a wheelchair. Her reason was she felt that once I sat down, I'd stay down, and I would not be able to walk. But I was still walking and using Carrie when I needed to if I was going to be on a long journey or someplace where there was a lot of walking to be done. My physical therapist said to me, 'Use things to help you and save the energy you need to do the things you want to do. If you use up your energy to walk somewhere when you get there, you're not going to have any fun.' They were right, so I started using Carrie, but I continued to walk for quite a while.

"Then I began having problems falling, and that's a scary, scary thing. I have a friend, Maria, and she's known people who had ALS in the past and she said, 'You know what, it's an opportunistic disease because it takes advantage of your weakness, and it'll give you other problems that you don't want. You have to always be cognizant of where you are and know what your obstacles are.'

"Carrie did a great service for me for quite a while, but in September 2019, I was bumped up to a power chair, which is quite elaborate. It's a 300- to 350-pound chair that has many functions. It'll take me up in the air if I need to be up in the air to reach something. It's quite comfortable. Once I got that chair, I was pretty much in that chair full time, which I still am; I use it every day. I call it Little Carrie because it's younger than my original Carrie.

"I am fortunate enough to be living at the beach, but getting on the beach became very difficult over the last two summers. My friend Cecile started a fundraiser with former colleagues and friends. They raised enough money to purchase a beach wheelchair for me, which is very, very helpful. It's a four-wheel drive chair. My son Chris named it Bad Larry the first time he saw it, and that name has stuck. It's a great tool. It gets me out on the beach, which I love. It keeps me independent and doing the things I want to do.

"My days now are very quiet. I sleep in most days. When I rise, we either watch TV or we go out shopping, pre-COVID-19. The pandemic has slowed that down, of course, quite a bit. From March 13, 2020, until the beginning of June I stayed pretty much in the house. I did take my dog, Ringo, around the neighborhood. We have great neighbors and we'd social distance with them. We'd wear masks, but it really slowed down our social life. We had already started doing video phone calls with friends and family in January.

"We were blessed with a grandchild, Claire Melanie, and our son Christopher and his wife Ashley are great parents. They video chat with us whenever they can, so we can watch her grow. Prior to the pandemic, we had visits, and now we've had a couple more. She's just the love of our life! We're so happy to have her!

"Our other son, Alex, and his wife Allyssa live in Las Vegas, and unfortunately, they haven't been able to get back to Massachusetts because of the pandemic. They were going to come out in the summertime for a wedding, but that didn't happen. We do miss them, but I talk to him quite often on the phone, and we video chat with them when we can. We're keeping in touch, but our days are pretty quiet.

"I enjoy the outside; I go out whenever I can. Sometimes it's warm, but I don't care. I'm going to go outside when I can, because soon it will be wintertime. Then it's cold, and I hate the cold. I much prefer ninety-degree days in the summer than thirty-degree days in the winter.

"The way I see it is you take what you're given, and you deal with it. Some people say the glass is half empty, and some people say the glass is half full, but I think it depends on what you do with what's in the glass. It's how you make your life as comfortable and as pleasant as possible.

"My days of traveling are probably over, because it's too hard to get on a plane. We can do road trips, but I'm happy here in my home; it's very comfortable. We have a lot of company whenever possible. And you know, life has definitely slowed down with the pandemic, but that'll pick back up again. We just live a comfortable life now and find you don't miss the things that you think you would miss.

"I have great memories, I have to say, traveling and doing all the fun stuff that we used to do, but we still are able to have fun. We spend time together now and we do the things that make us happy now: enjoy a good movie, or I listen to audiobooks. It's quiet, but it's nice. I'm fortunate to have a husband who's very good to me. Taking care of me has become his priority. He's a great cook, I have to say, and will do anything for me.

"My disease seems to be progressing still at a slow pace. Thank goodness, though I am using a BiPap machine at night now to help with breathing. What it does is it saves energy with my diaphragm, so that I'm not struggling to breathe; that's a great thing. It takes some getting used to, but you adjust to it.

"I have a bed that adjusts and has a zero-gravity setting, which is great. It's the little things that make you comfortable and keep you happy, and I am happy. I look forward to many more visits with friends and family and seeing my granddaughter grow and just making the best of the situation you are dealt.

"Throughout my life, I heard my mother say that things can always be worse. You could consider that as being a negative way to look at things, but when you break it down, it's not negative. It's actually a positive way to look at things, because you do the best with what you have.

"For me, my current situation with my diagnosis would be a lot worse if I didn't have the love and care from dear friends and family, like my friend MaryRose who has been here twice at a moment's notice when Al was not well enough to care for me. Or the ability to stay in touch with my former coworkers, who have been very kind. And, of course, things would be a lot worse if Al had succumbed to his illness. He's my rock, and he takes care of me. When I'm down, he brings me up, and when I'm scared, he comforts me. So, I have to say, right now I'm living the happiest life that I can.

"I do that with peace and love, a lot of hope...and a splash or two of Chardonnay."

FINAL THOUGHTS

The ALS Ice Bucket Challenge changed the way nonprofits must think about using social media, whether they are large or small. If you had asked me if I thought the phenomenon could happen again, I probably would have said no. However, what happened with the Minnesota Freedom Fund in June 2020 has changed my mind. The confluence of what was happening regarding the media, politics, the COVID-19 pandemic, and the reinvigorated Black Lives Matter movement resulted in people's wanting to do something, anything. The requests for donations to a variety of nonprofits, including the MFF, was a call to action many people could understand and wanted to support. Sharing your donation and asking for others to help took place on social media. In the future, I will be interested to see if it can happen again.

I want to leave you with a few thoughts on how nonprofits receive funding and how they use the funds. One of the biggest challenges nonprofits face is fundraising, through donations, grants, and sometimes government contracts. I'm going to focus on general donations because I hope to explain why I chose to give the profits from this book to Compassionate Care ALS in Falmouth, Massachusetts, versus choosing to fund further research for ALS.

Every nonprofit needs to fund operations, the day-to-day costs of running an organization. These include rent, insurance, utilities, internet, salaries, and more. Without covering these costs, the nonprofit would not be able to open its doors to serve its mission. When you make a charitable gift to the nonprofit that is not restricted, the nonprofit can determine what it wants to do with the funding, including covering overhead costs. If you choose to restrict your donation to a scholarship fund, for example, it can only be used to cover scholarships. Now, there is nothing wrong with either of these donations, but I want you to know that nonprofits often struggle to cover overhead costs, which affects their ability to provide services. If you can't keep the doors open, you can't help people.

I spoke with Ron Hoffman, executive director of Compassionate Care ALS, about the need to provide funding for immediate care, as we both think it is an important facet of supporting people with ALS, but also of many other nonprofits that have clients with immediate needs. He said, "Our work is about tending to and caring for individuals navigating the complexities of their disease. The resources that requires, it's large. My wish is that individuals with means, who are supporting the world of research, could *see the importance of putting some of those dollars into care*. There are a lot of people out there who are suffering a great deal. We fill a niche in their care that is not being filled by anyone else."

The work involved in caring for someone with ALS is difficult but can also be rewarding, given support and encouragement. Hoffman noted, "It's more than just raising awareness; it's touching people hearts. There's room for families living with an illness like ALS and their caregivers to really transform their lives to see things in a completely different way—to grow and to evolve. It's all about compassion, real compassion—the ability to show up, be present, listen, bear witness. Sometimes, beauty can occur. I've seen people seriously transform their lives and awaken in some way that was completely new to them. It's been truly inspirational."

One of the reasons I chose Compassionate Care ALS (CCALS) to receive the proceeds from this book was because the organization requires little in the way of paperwork for a family to receive support. For many with ALS, navigating the complexities of MassHealth, Medicare, or Medicaid can be overwhelming. They don't have time for more applications and paperwork. Hoffman meets with his families to find out how he can help. He said, "I'd rather have a simple conversation than worry about forms and paperwork. 'What do you need, what are your expenses?' If I can help with expenses, then I will. Sometimes, that's all we do for a family—but that alone transforms their experience."

Many of the families are surprised by this. Hoffman noted, "I don't have time for bureaucratic red tape. My families don't need the added burden of another complex application." Hoffman has worked with families to provide wheelchair ramps and other medical equipment to help them maintain as much independence and dignity as possible.

Hoffman also sees the role of CCALS as an organization that provides training to those in the medical field and hospice organizations. They offer programs that help people working with patients better understand the patient's experience. Hoffman shared, "The end of our life should be equally as important as the beginning of our life. Birth and death are equally sacred. We were birthed into this world, and the majority of the time there's great education around the birth process. But when it comes to dying, there's not much preparation for it. That's one of the things that we're able to bring to the table, for those wanting to explore dying. That's an incredibly large part of my work, and there's nothing more important."

When Hoffman talked about this, I remembered my late husband saying, "We're all dying; some of us are just closer to it than others." It is true that as a society, we do not do well talking about death and our expectations around that process. An organization like CCALS provides people with the opportunity to explore their thoughts on the process of death and dying.

In the case of CCALS and many other nonprofit organizations, people must understand that donating to a nonprofit to help keep the lights on is just as important as donating to research, and it has an immediate effect on improving one's quality of life. Yes, research is important and needed, but so is support for those living with ALS, families included.

Your support by buying this book helps CCALS provide training, services, and equipment for those diagnosed with ALS. Its mission:

> Compassionate Care ALS (CCALS) is a nonprofit organization with a mission to support people diagnosed with ALS, their families, healthcare providers, and communities as they navigate the complexities, both physical and emotional, associated with the disease. The organization provides resources including equipment, educational opportunities, Medicare/Medicaid assistance, communication assistance, guidance and awareness with regards to living with ALS, caregiving, and exploring end-of-life when invited. CCALS offers an innovative approach to delivering support and services to our clients, which we tailor to the needs of each individual and their support network.[87]

If you would like to learn more, or make a personal donation, please visit www.ccals.org.

---

87 Compassionate Care ALS, "Mission Statement," accessed September 25, 2020.

ACKNOWLEDGEMENTS OF MELANIE ST. CROIX

First, I must thank Deb Finch for including my story in her project. Her concern for my well-being never wavered. The end result is a testament to her hard work and determination.

In addition, I would like to thank:

The multidisciplinary patient care team at Lahey Hospital in Burlington for their commitment to exceptional care.

The many staff members at Lahey Hospital who have cared for my husband over the years and kept him going.

The ALS Association of Northern New England and Massachusetts chapters for their commitment to advocacy, care, and a cure. A special thanks to Laurie McFarren of the Northern New England Chapter. Laurie is resourceful, caring, and always there to help navigate the pitfalls of this horrible disease.

My "funamish" family, MaryRose, Don, Tina, Mike, Lisa, and Ed, for years of love and support and always keeping the laughs going.

My mother, Marilyn Murphy, for keeping hope alive through prayer.

Family and friends for keeping me in their thoughts and staying connected.

My former coworkers, whom I am proud to call friends, at the Lowell Five for their unwavering love and support.

My dear friends and girls' weekend companions, Jodi, Eileen, and Jill, for all the laughs and adventures on our trips.

My son Christopher for all his advice and technical support, along with my amazing daughter-in-law Ashley for the gift of our delightful granddaughter, Claire Melanie.

My son Alex and wonderful daughter-in-law Allyssa for their love and support across the miles.

My Ocean Angel, Janice, for helping to make my ocean dreams come true.

The wonderful people who consistently supported the Pepperell Music Center.

My Ogunquit neighbors who have become my friends.

And most of all, my amazing husband, Alan, whose devotion and care keep me going.

APPENDIX

INTRODUCTION

ALS Association. "ALS Ice Bucket Challenge Year-End Update: Over $94 Million in Commitments Since 2014." January 30, 2018. Accessed April 4, 2020. *https://www.als.org/stories-news/als-ice-bucket-challenge-year-end-update-over-94-million-commitments-2014.*

Gilbert, Nan. *A Dog for Joey.* New York: Harper & Row, 1967.

Kander, Diana. *All In Startup: Launching a New Idea When Everything is on the Line.* Hoboken: John Wiley & Sons, Inc., 2014.

Kopp, Wendy. *One Day, All Children...: The Unlikely Triumph Of Teach For America And What I Learned Along The Way.* Cambridge: Perseus Books, 2013.

Trejos, Amanda. "Ice Bucket Challenge: 5 things you should know." *USA Today.* July 3, 2017. *https://www.usatoday.com/story/news/2017/07/03/ice-bucket-challenge-5-things-you-should-know/448006001/.*

CHAPTER 1

ALSA. "What is ALS?" Accessed April 6, 2020. *http://www.alsa.org/about-als/what-is-als.html.*

Mayo Clinic. "Crohn's Disease." Accessed April 30, 2020. *https://www.mayoclinic.org/diseases-conditions/crohns-disease/symptoms-causes/syc-20353304.*

Frates, Pete. "New Book Reveals the Inspiring Story Behind the Ice Bucket Challenge." TODAY, November 3, 2017. Video 5:22. *https://www.youtube.com/watch?v=uqGF8GAuYRo.*

CHAPTER 2

Duffin, Erin. "Revenues of reporting nonprofit organizations in the U.S. from 1998 to 2016." Statista.com. August 30, 2016. Accessed September 6, 2020. *https://www.statista.com/statistics/250878/number-of-foundations-in-the-united-states/.*

Giving in America: Toward a Stronger Voluntary Sector: Report of the Commission on Private Philanthropy and Public Needs. United States: The Commission. Accessed June 27, 2020. *https://archives.iupui.edu/handle/2450/889.*

Hammack, David. *Making the Nonprofit Sector in the United States.* Bloomington: Indiana University Press, 1998.

McKeever, Brice. "The Nonprofit Sector in Brief 2018: Public Charities, Giving and Volunteering." Urban Institute: National Center for Charitable Statistics. December 13, 2018. *https://nccs.urban.org/publication/nonprofit-sector-brief-2018#the-nonprofit-sector-in-brief-2018-public-charites-giving-and-volunteering.*

Muslic, Hana. A Brief History of Nonprofit Organizations (And What We Can Learn). *Nonprofit Hub.* October 27, 2017. *https://nonprofithub.org/starting-a-nonprofit/a-brief-history-of-nonprofit-organizations/.*

Orson, Diane. "Millennials and Charitable Giving: A New Approach To Philanthropy." National Public Radio, December 27, 2019. Accessed September 19, 2020. *https://www.wnpr.org/post/millennials-and-charitable-giving-new-approach-philanthropy.*

Pruszewicz, Aleksandra and VanderHulst, Angela. n.d. Key Dates and Events in American Philanthropic History 1815 to Present. Accessed April 23, 2020. *https://www.learningtogive.org/resources/key-dates-and-events-american-philanthropic-history-1815-present.*

Putnam, Robert J. *Bowling Alone: The Collapse and Revival of American Community.* New York: Simon & Schuster, 2000.

Salamon, Lester M., Chelsea L. Newhouse, Chelsea L., and S. Wojciech Sokolowski. January 2019. "The 2018 Nonprofit Employment Report." Johns Hopkins Center for Civil Society Studies. *http://ccss.jhu.edu/wp-content/uploads/downloads/2019/01/2019-NP-Employment-Report_FINAL_1.8.2019.pdf.*

Worth, Michael J. *Nonprofit Management: Principles and Practice.* Thousand Oaks: SAGE Publications, Inc., 2014.

CHAPTER 3

Acs, Zoltan J. *Why Philanthropy Matters: How the Wealthy Give, and What It Means for Our Economic Well-Being.* Princeton, New Jersey: Princeton University Press, 2013.

Andrew Carnegie Biography. Biography.com Editors. June 24, 2019. Accessed April 25, 2020. *https://www.biography.com/business-figure/andrew-carnegie.*

Arnsberger, Paul, Melissa Ludlum, Margaret Riley, and Mark Stanton. A History of the Tax-Exempt Sector: An SOI Perspective.

2008. Accessed April 26, 2020. *https://www.irs.gov/pub/irs-soi/tehistory.pdf.*

Capps, Kriston. "How Andrew Carnegie Built the Architecture of American Literacy." *Bloomberg CityLab.* October 28, 2014. *https://www.bloomberg.com/news/articles/2014-10-28/how-andrew-carnegie-built-the-architecture-of-american-literacy.*

Carnegie, Andrew. The Gospel of Wealth. 1889. Accessed April 28, 2020. *https://production-carnegie.s3.amazonaws.com/filer_public/ab/c9/abc9fb4b-dc86-4ce8-ae31-a983b9a326ed/ccny_essay_1889_thegospelofwealth.pdf.*

EyeWitness to History. "Andrew Carnegie Becomes a Capitalist, 1856." 2007. Accessed April 25, 2020. *http://www.eyewitnesstohistory.com/carnegie.htm.*

Rosalsky, Greg. "Charitable Giving Is Down. It Might Be Time To Reform The Charitable Deduction." *Planet Money.* November 12, 2019. *https://www.npr.org/sections/money/2019/11/12/778326512/charitable-giving-is-down-it-might-be-time-to-reform-the-charitable-deduction.*

CHAPTER 4

American Cancer Society. "Healthy blood donors needed during Coronavirus outbreak." March 13, 2020. Video, 0:30. *https://www.youtube.com/watch?v=Wl2mt4ZFYRA.*

Goodworld (blog). "Tagging Peer to Peer Giving on Facebook." August 18, 2018. Accessed April 5, 2020. *https://blog.goodworld.me/tagging-peer-to-peer-giving-on-facebook-94ce3420d2bf.*

Harman, Wade. "5 Psychology Tips to Improve Your Social Media Posts." *Social Media Examiner.* October 7, 2015. *https://www.socialmediaexaminer.com/5-psychology-tips-to-improve-your-social-media-posts/.*

Morand, Tatiana. "The Ultimate Nonprofit Video Marketing Strategy + 5 of the Best Nonprofit Videos We've Seen." *Wild Apricot* (blog). July 20, 2018. *https://www.wildapricot.com/blogs/newsblog/2018/07/20/nonprofit-video-marketing-strategy.*

CHAPTER 5

Campbell, Julia. *How to Build and Mobilize A Social Media Community for Your Nonprofit in 90 Days.* Lexington: Bold & Bright Media, LLC, 2020.

Dunham+Company and Marketing Support Network. *"Nonprofit Social Media Scorecard | A National Study Analyzing the Social Media Habits of Nonprofits."* (2015). Accessed May 7, 2020. *https://www.marketingsupportnetwork.com/wp-content/uploads/2015/11/Social-Media-Scorecard.pdf.*

CHAPTER 6

ALS Therapy Development Institute, "Quinn for the Win." Accessed September 27, 2020. *https://www.als.net/affiliate/quinn-for-the-win/.*

Berger, Jonah. "'Contagious': Jonah Berger on Why Things Catch On." March 13, 2013. In Knowledge@Wharton. Podcast Transcript. P2. *https://knowledge.wharton.upenn.edu/ article/contagious-jonah-berger-on-why-things-catch-on/.*

Demetri, George. Public Funding is the Lifeblood of Cancer Research. *CancerTodayMag.* December 21, 2018. *https://www.cancertodaymag.org/Pages/Winter2018-2019/Public-Funding-is-the-Lifeblood-of-Cancer-Research.aspx.*

Frates, Pete. "My Journey from Baseball Star to ALS Patient, 75 Years After Lou Gehrig." *Bleacherreport,* July 2, 2014. *https://bleacherreport.com/articles/2109533-my-journey-from-baseball-star-to-als-patient-75-years-after-lou-gehrig.*

Messina, Chris. "On a Mission to Make Myself Useful." Accessed June 9, 2020. *https://chrismessina.me/.*

Panko, Ben. "A Decade Ago, the Hashtag Reshaped the Internet." *Smithsonian.* August 23, 2017. *https://www.smithsonianmag.com/smart-news/decade-ago-hashtag-reshaped-internet-180964605/.*

Protalinski, Emil. "Facebook passes 1.19 billion monthly active users, 874 million mobile users, and 728 million daily users." *TheNextWeb.* Oct 30, 2013. *https://thenextweb.com/facebook/2013/10/ 30/facebook-passes-1-19-billion-monthly-active-users-874-million-mobile-users-728-million-daily-users/.*

Reddy, Sumathi. "How the Ice-Bucket Challenge Got Its Start." *Wall Street Journal,* August 14, 2014. *https://www.wsj.com/articles/how-the-ice-bucket-challenge-got-its-start-1408049557.*

Sherman, Casey and Dave Wedge. *The Ice Bucket Challenge: Pete Frates and the Fight against ALS.* Lebanon: University Press of New England, 2014.

Sifferlin, Alexandra. "Here's How the ALS Ice Bucket Challenge Actually Started." *Time.* August 18, 2014. *https://time.com/3136507/als-ice-bucket-challenge-started/.*

Widrich, Leo. "Social Media in 2013: User Demographics for Twitter, Facebook, Pinterest and Instagram." *Buffer* (blog). May 2, 2013. *https://buffer.com/resources/social-media-in-2013-user-demographics-for-twitter-facebook-pinterest-and-instagram.*

Wynne, Robert. "There Are No Guarantees—Or Exact Statistics—For Going Viral." *Forbes.* March 9, 2018. *https://www.forbes.com/sites/robertwynne/2018/03/09/there-are-no-guarantees-or-exact-statistics-for-going-viral/#54439fac5e8c.*

CHAPTER 7

Cooper, Paige and Shannon Tien. "How to Create a Social Media Content Calendar: Tips and Templates." *Hootsuite Social Media Management* (Blog). January 27, 2020. *https://blog.hootsuite.com/how-to-create-a-social-media-content-calendar/.*

Duane, Margot. "Nonprofit Photography: Ethics and Approaches." *The Community Network*. Accessed June 16, 2020. *https://storytelling.comnetwork.org/explore/102/nonprofit-photography-ethics-and-approaches.*

Panjwani, Sameer. "12 Months Of Content Event Triggers For Your Editorial Calendar." *Search Engine People* (Blog). December 9, 2014. *https://www.searchenginepeople.com/blog/925-event-content-calendar.html.*

CHAPTER 8

Campbell, Julia. "How to Create A Culture of Storytelling in Your Nonprofit." CauseVox (Blog). Accessed June 16, 2020. *https://www.causevox.com/blog/nonprofit-culture-storytelling/.*

Dixon, Julie. "Building a Storytelling Culture." *Stanford Social Innovation Review*, October 27, 2014. *https://ssir.org/articles/entry/building_a_storytelling_culture.*

Stanton, Brandon. "Humans of New York-About." Humans of New York. Accessed September 30, 2020. *https://www.humansofnewyork.com/*

Rees, Sandy. "How You Can Use Nonprofit Storytelling to Increase Donations and Involvement." *Get Fully Funded*. June 18, 2019. *https://getfullyfunded.com/nonprofit-storytelling/.*

CHAPTER 9

Agnes, Melissa. "Detecting A Social Media Crisis vs. A Social Media Issue." September 26, 2012. Accessed 5/24/20. *https://melissaagnes.com/detecting-a-social-media-crisis-vs-a-social-media-issue/.*

Friedenthal, Andrew. "What's Your Nonprofit Social Media Crisis Response Plan?" Software Advice. May 16, 2018. Accessed May 18, 2020. *https://www.softwareadvice.com/resources/nonprofit-social-media-crisis-response/.*

Kanter, Beth. "Two Examples of Nonprofit Social Media That Will Make You Smile (and learn a best practice or two)." Oct. 4, 2017. Accessed 4/24/20. *http://www.bethkanter.org/sm-best-practices/.*

Leimkuehler, Katie. "The Red Cross Rogue Tweet: How to Turn a Social Media Mistake into a Positive Outcome." *CPrime* (blog) 11/22/2016. Accessed 5/24/20. *https://aspetraining.com/resources/blog/red-cross-rogue-tweet-how-to-turn-a-social-media-mistake-into-a-positive-outcome.*

CRISIS PLAN LINKS:

https://www.wildapricot.com/blogs/newsblog/2020/03/20/nonprofit-crisis-communications-plan

https://images.template.net/wp-content/uploads/2015/09/11153653/Social-Media-Crisis-Action-Plan-for-Non-Profit-PDF.pdf

https://www.michiganfoundations.org/resources/crisis-communication-plan-nonprofit-toolkit

https://sustainingplaces.files.wordpress.com/2014/03/crisiscomm.pdf

CHAPTER 10

Sherman, Casey and Wedge, Dave. *The Ice Bucket Challenge: Pete Frates and the Fight against ALS*. Lebanon, NH: University Press of New England, 2017.

CHAPTER 11

ALS Association. "Ice Bucket Challenge dramatically accelerated the fight against ALS." Press Release. June 4, 2019. Accessed September 13, 2020. *https://www.als.org/stories-news/ice-bucket-challenge-dramatically-accelerated-fight-against-als.*

Hrywna, Mark. "Unrest Spurs $30 Million To Minnesota Freedom Fund." *The Nonprofit Times*, June 8, 2020. *https://www.thenonprofittimes.com/fundraising/unrest-spurs-30-million-to-minnesota-freedom-fund/.*

EPILOGUE

Compassionate Care ALS. "Mission Statement." Accessed September 25, 2020. *https://ccals.org/mission-and-history/.*

Made in the USA
Middletown, DE
15 December 2020

28417108R00106